With love   from

Mum

Christ▯

Finding Stefan:
Colin's Story

– HAZEL HARTSTONE –

To Colin

Best wishes,

Hazel Hartstone

http://www.fast-print.net/bookshop

FINDING STEFAN: COLIN'S STORY

Copyright © Hazel Hartstone 2015

The right of Hazel Hartstone to be identified as the author of this work has
been asserted by her in accordance with the Copyright, Designs and
Patents Act 1988 and any subsequent amendments thereto.

A catalogue record for this book is available from the British Library

ISBN 978-178456-283-0

First published 2015 by
FASTPRINT PUBLISHING
Peterborough, England.

Prologue

About three years before my father died in 1993, he wrote about his life on a ruled foolscap pad. He gave me these pages, one by one, and I typed them up on an old-fashioned typewriter. It was a revelation to me, as I knew he'd had an extraordinary life, but as I typed, I read things he had never talked about, and it seemed part of another world.

After my mother died in 2008, I found these pages tucked away in a cupboard, along with letters, postcards and photographs from his time in Poland during the Second World War.

I thought about what my father had written all those years before and, as a tribute to him and the Polish people who helped him, I decided to turn it into a book.

Full Circle

He gave me a powerful shove and slammed the door. Trapped, there was no way out. I dropped down onto the heap of coal in despair. In a few days' time I'd have been free and on my way back to England, back to the one who had kept my spirit alive for the last four years, but why pretend any more? Tomorrow I'd be dead. The German bullet I'd expected for so long would arrive. Would anyone miss me or had everyone forgotten? Had my wife found someone else? Now I'd never know. Of one thing I was sure: my Polish friends would never forget me. I imagined the wooden cross they would put on my grave, *Stefan Wysocki – Nie Mowe*. Thank God, they were not involved; at least I'd not let them down. There must have been times when they thought I might.

Early Days

My earliest recollection came to mind, another escape that went wrong, although at the age of four the consequences weren't so grave.

On a bright spring morning in 1918 I was bundled into the back of an ambulance, suffering with scarlet fever and taken to Mastin Moor Isolation Hospital, along roads not much better than a farm track. After a few days of confinement, I decided to try to find my way home. I succeeded but Ma promptly returned me, and I had to stay for the next two weeks. My home was in the small Derbyshire mining village of Stanfree. A zinc bath hung on the wall outside nearly every back door. We had a living room, sitting room and scullery. Upstairs there were two bedrooms: one I shared with my sister Winnie and our parents, and our lodger, Ernest Ballinger, had the other. Three sisters, May, Violet and Erma, and two brothers, Arthur and Harold, slept in the attic. Harold and Arthur worked at the local pit. Erma had a disability with her legs; she walked on her toes with her feet turned a little inwards. I hardly ever saw my elder sisters because as they left school, they went into service as kitchen maids or cooks and lived away from home. I don't remember growing up with them, yet they would often relate how they sailed me on the Staveley Canal in a tin bath. Apparently the bath sank and my father jumped in and fetched me out.

I hope their story was true because that was the only thing he ever did for me.

My father and his elder brother Harry spent their early years in Sheffield workhouse after their mother died, and then they went to live with their grandmother. Uncle Harry became a master cutler and my father a cobbler, but somehow he drifted into coalmining. He'd been a smart well-made man in his younger days, but I only remember him with his legs permanently bent at the knees, the result of a pit accident. Sometimes I felt sorry for him, but at least once a week when he rolled home drunk, I loathed him.

The two dominant people in my life were my mother and Ernest Ballinger. My mother, brought up with four brothers, was prepared to stand up and fight. Ballinger was a clever man and he said that education took you beyond the need to fight. He taught me to read and write, and while we went for long walks, he explained things to me.

As the time drew near for me to start school, I received conflicting advice. Ma said I must stand up for myself and never run away, and Ballinger would tell me not to get into scrapes, keep my head down and concentrate on learning.

Before the end of the first school term, I developed appendicitis. The doctor said, as I was so young, it could be 'swilled away'. He advised, 'Keep him away from school, give him plenty of exercise and keep him on this special diet.'

Ballinger saw to it that I had a long walk almost every day, but the diet! We either ate or we didn't, there was no money for anything special. Wages in the coalmines were very poor and my father, because of his disability, was unable to command top wages. Fortunately, my mother could turn her hand to anything: cleaning, decorating and nursing.

During that summer, I was busy running errands for neighbours who couldn't do their own shopping and, for a five-year-old, I started saving quite a lot of money. Ballinger felt I was wasting my time running errands. To him money was second to education.

This new activity brought me in contact with more people and it brought a dark cloud into my life. There came a time when I had more errands than I could manage and when I refused a neighbour, she called me 'Little Ballinger'. I thought this was because Ballinger was so good to me and took an interest in everything I did. I had a surprise one day when another woman called me 'Ballinger'. I asked her why and her retort was, 'Because he's your bloody father.' The full implication of that didn't occur to me at that early age, I just felt confused. I daren't tell my mother, she would have gone and flattened the woman, so I told Ballinger. I was disappointed, he didn't explain, he just said, 'Colin, people can be very cruel, especially to children. Take no notice of what they say.'

Unexpectedly, my mother announced we were moving house, no one knew why. Our new home was on the outskirts of the village up a lonely lane. I was over the moon; it was a young boy's dream. A row of six houses in the middle of nowhere, they called it 'Sunny Banks'.

Every day as I went to school I passed the pithead. Sometimes I'd stop and watch while the cage dropped like a stone. Someday I'd be dropping down there, unless I listened to Ballinger. It was a common sight to see injured men carried from the pit. We children would ask what had happened; mostly it was a fall of dirt or a fall of coal. When I told Ma she would say, 'Men's backs are cheaper than supports.' I was growing up with fear in my heart and this became more intense.

One day when I returned from school, my mother wasn't at home. Winnie announced, 'Ma's gone to Mrs Ward's house and you haven't to go there.'

The Ward family lived in a cottage in Oxcroft Wood. I loved to visit them and it seemed strange saying I wasn't to go. Curiosity got the better of me and I was soon running through the wood. When I reached the cottage, surprisingly, all the blinds were drawn. There was no answer when I knocked, so I tried the door.

'Well, what have you come for?' my mother asked. My eyes went to the table. My mother was stitching a white sheet round a body.

'Who is it?' I stammered.

'Mr Ward was buried under a fall. This is what you've to look forward to when you go down the pit.'

Normally I was loath to leave that cottage in the wood, with a lovely swing hanging from a chestnut tree, but that day I couldn't leave soon enough. That scene remained in my thoughts for weeks.

When I was nearly six years old, and in spite of everything, the appendix problem remained. That was until one day when I was going to Clowne on an errand. I fainted in the street and someone carried me into their house and sent for the doctor. I knew nothing until I woke up in a strange bed in Sheffield hospital. Everyone was dressed in white; I thought they were angels. What a relief when I saw someone dressed in blue. This was different from the isolation hospital at Mastin Moor. I was treated like a lord; I could have stayed there forever.

The headmistress of Stanfree Infants' School was Mrs Woodhouse. She was an angel with golden hair and the children worshipped her. Even though I missed a lot of schooling through illness, she never bothered me. 'It's obvious someone at home is interested in you,' she said.

After Stanfree, everyone moved on to Shuttlewood Junior School, a mile away. What a difference. It seemed to annoy the headmaster that, no matter how much time I was absent from school, I was always in the top four of the class. He wanted to know who was teaching me at home and he caned me at every opportunity. I tried not to get into too many scrapes at school but there was just once when I thought my courage had gone a little too far.

Walking through a neighbouring village, I passed a group of men sitting on the grass verge playing cards. One of them called to me and I turned round. He was six feet tall, weighed about eighteen stones and was the village layabout. I went back and asked him what he wanted.

'Is Ballinger yer dad?' he jeered.

There was a building brick lying on the ground. I picked it up and all the men jumped up and moved out of the way. This big man just stood there. 'If ya throw that, yer'll be forrit,' he shouted.

I hurled it at him with all the strength I could muster. He turned as he saw it coming and it hit him in the middle of his back. He went down like a log. I turned and ran, scared for my life. I avoided that village like the plague after that.

A few weeks later, I dashed out of school, ran around a bunch of boys and collided with the same man on the pavement. He held me by the shoulders. My heart missed a beat as I recognised his huge frame. Holding me at arm's length, he looked at me and said, 'Tha'rs a funny lad, a didn'a think thar'd throw that brick.' He let me go and I went as fast as my trembling legs would take me.

The year of 1925 was a very eventful year. Uncle Harry came to visit and the following weekend he brought his wife, Kate. I'd never met them and I imagined they were posh people because he was a master cutler and owned his own shop. What I didn't know at that time was, when the weather was good, he would shut the shop to go tramping with his wife. They smoked clay pipes, drank like fishes and swore like troupers. Uncle Harry brought lovely cutlery that he'd made, but on the way, he would call in public houses and sell his wares to buy drink.

He arrived and placed a big brown paper parcel on the table.

'Look what your Uncle Harry has brought for you,' said my father. I was curious; I thought it was a present.

'Ugh!' the smell nearly knocked me over. It was a parcel of meat from the 'Rag and Tag' market in Sheffield and it looked as if it was ready to walk back.

After about four of these weekends, Ballinger left. He couldn't stand them. I'll never forget when he packed all his books in a tin trunk. He said sadly, 'If you ever need me or any of these, you know where I'm going.' He went to lodge with a Salvation Army family, very different from Aunt Kate.

A few months later, matters came to a head. My mother had already said, 'If they come again, I'm leaving.' One Saturday night, Uncle Harry and Aunt Kate arrived again worse for drink, and I heard my mother give them the ultimatum. Curiously, I was never worried about my mother, I always felt sure she could look after herself. I heard my mother come upstairs and I crept into her bedroom. She was packing a case.

'What about us Ma?' I asked.

'You'll be alright, I'll get in touch with you,' she said gently.

I couldn't understand her going quietly; it seemed very out of character. I heard the door open and close and I broke down and cried. A few minutes later all hell seemed to break loose, I knew my mother was back. There was screaming and shouting, and then the door slammed. I felt better; at least my mother had left under her true colours.

There was Father, my disabled sister Erma and me in a home that died. Erma and I were quite capable of looking after the housework and the cooking, but there was no organisation. Father had no idea how to shop, so we had mostly makeshift meals.

After two weeks my eldest sister May arrived on the scene. She had been married for about six or seven years, had two young sons and they lived in two rented rooms. Work was hard and difficult to get in those days and her husband wasn't fond of work, therefore landlords thought twice about letting them a house. She offered to come and look after us, but when I asked if she meant daily, she said, 'No, we'll come and live with you.'

It was the easiest way out, but to me it was the closing of the door. I argued, but it was no use and a few days later my sister May and her family moved in. During the next few weeks, I realised why she'd always looked thin and pale; she was starving herself to feed her husband and children. Father started taking an interest in food. He sent me shopping to Clowne to buy meat, but we saw little of it. Ernest, my brother-in-law had the lion's share.

I noticed Father putting on his collar and tie instead of a muffler when he went out at the weekend. I knew he was trying to find Ma, but to me it was pointless.

She would never come back while my sister and family were living with us.

One Saturday night Father didn't come home, but the next day he appeared like his old self, drunk as a lord. He had found out where Ma was living and she'd agreed to come home if he found somewhere else for us to rent.

We left 'Sunny Banks' to live in Clowne, sharing a house with a widow and her three children. I believe the only reason the widow took us in was because my father had an allowance of coal from the pit, and she was able to share it. Nevertheless, I was happy; my mother was home.

In 1926, there was talk of a strike. We were still living in two rooms when the strike started and it was probably as well since we only had a voucher for thirteen shillings a week, to exchange for groceries to feed four of us.

For the boys, it was an exciting time at first. It wasn't until later some bitterness crept in. The blacklegs who went to work had a police escort and if the men on strike did much in the way of picketing, they were soon in trouble. A crowd of boys would accompany the procession to the pit gates banging a stick on tin cans; we called it 'ran-tanning'.

During this time, the soup kitchens kept us alive. It was there we had our main meal of the day and sometimes the only meal.

One day when I returned from school, I smelt something burning. Ma had a good fire going in the grate, but the smell was terrible.

'What is it?' I asked.

'I'm burning your dad's pit clothes and I'll burn him if he mentions going to work.'

I read the note on the table advising him to go to work, since in view of his disability, they probably wouldn't be able to find him suitable employment later on. It made me feel sick. My father walked with his legs permanently bent; his hand was stiff, he could neither open nor close it, both were the results of accidents in the pit. I was too young to understand politics, in fact, we only had a vague idea what the strike was all about and to us it was a big adventure. Unfortunately, not everyone viewed it in that respect, as I soon found out.

One Sunday evening I arrived at church to sing in the choir and my surplus wasn't on the peg. None of the other boys had seen it, so I asked the choirmaster if he knew where it was.

'You won't need it,' he said and added, 'we don't want boys here who go and sing *The Red Flag.*'

I soon realised what had happened. During the previous week, there had been a meeting in the Miners' Welfare and children were allowed to accompany their parents. Ma took me with her and after the meeting closed, they sang *The Red Flag.* Everyone knew the chorus, but when it came to the verse, no one knew it. I stood up and sang the verses and everyone joined in the chorus. They applauded me and I felt so proud. I'd sung a song and at that time, it meant nothing else to me.

Now many things started passing through my mind. The country seemed to me divided between the haves and the have-nots. The choirmaster was right: they couldn't have boys who had sung that song, when the first three rows of the congregation were the haves.

As I walked home, terribly disappointed because I enjoyed being in the choir, I thought if only the first three rows of the congregation go to heaven, there won't be much work done up there.

The strike dragged on. Everyone was confident the workers were winning. It was the nineteenth week when suddenly there was a change. I asked my mother what was happening. She said, 'We're being sold down the river and we're going to suffer more than most.'

Her words meant nothing to me at that time, but later on, I was to remember them. The strike ended and the workers had lost. There was one crumb of comfort for my family. Apparently, there was to be no victimisation. How hollow those words seemed to me as week after week my father went down to the colliery looking for work and was told, 'Come and see me next week Alfie, I might have something for you then.' Although I'd no love for him, at times I could have cried as I saw him waddling like a duck down the road. His lameness always showed more when he was tired and three miles to Oxcroft colliery and three miles back was no joke to a lame man.

I started my paper round again after the strike, and the newsagent, Mr Calow, knowing how things were at home, gave me a morning round before school started as well. Two days a week I went round from door to door selling kippers and bloaters for a local fishmonger; it was hard work carrying a big basket and my sides were red raw, but we certainly needed the money.

While on my round one day, I knocked on a door and was surprised when Ernest Ballinger opened it. His first question was typical of him, 'Why aren't you at school?'

I told him because my father was unemployed after the strike; I had to do something to help.

'You'll regret it one day,' he said and he gave me ten shillings and told me to visit him again.

Ma was furious. 'We don't want charity. You can take it back.'

I felt so annoyed and replied, 'No I won't. How can I take back all that Ballinger has given and done for me in the past?'

We needed every penny because although no one expected payment during the strike, it was different now it was over.

The woman we lodged with pushed a note under the door saying: *Thirty-four weeks' rent, now due.* No one could understand that the strike wasn't over for us.

By the time Father had been off work for nearly a year, the conditions we lived in became unbelievable. The woman whose house we lived in refused to let us fetch water from her kitchen tap, so we carried every drop of water from a neighbour's house. We cooked all our food on a small gas ring. Ma asked the council to find us a house, but the main drawback was Father being out of work.

Our luck seemed to change all at once. The errand boy from the colliery brought a note that read: *Alfie, start work tonight, without fail – Archie Gray*.

Father started work that night and when he returned next morning, he told us what had happened. The under-manager had gone on his fortnight holiday and Archie Gray, who was an overman, took over while he was away. He had often thought about my father and this was his opportunity to do something about it.

Ma asked Father to wait for his bath until I'd taken a note to the doctor asking him to call. When the doctor arrived, he enquired who was ill.

'All of us. We're sick to death of living like this,' Ma replied.

He looked round the room. There was Father with the pit dirt still on his face and the zinc bath on the floor ready for his bath.

'Do you all live in this one room?' he asked.

'No, we sleep upstairs, but we fetch water from the neighbours and carry all the waste water right round the block to the drain.'

He sat down and wrote a letter. 'Take this to the council and if you haven't got a house in a week come and see me.'

A week later, we received a house. It was like starting a new life, two bedrooms upstairs, two rooms downstairs and a bathroom and toilet. I couldn't wait to have a bath with hot and cold water. I'd never had a bath in a bathroom before. The lights fascinated me; I only knew oil or gas lamps. Ma had to stop me switching them on and off.

Things were picking up now; I was even able to buy a second-hand bicycle with my paper-round money.

Starting Work

T ime seemed to fly, it was the summer of 1927 and I was leaving school at Christmas, but I didn't know what I was going to do. After making a few enquiries around the farms and getting some sarcastic remarks about my size, I gave up. Most of the other boys were going down the pit, but not me. Although I didn't need it, I had another reminder of the dangers down there.

A group of us were going home from school at midday for dinner, when we saw dozens of men hurrying down the road. We dashed up to the pit gates to hear the mine was flooded. The boys, whose fathers or brothers worked there, started rushing around to find out if anyone was still underground. Later, an announcement informed us that everyone was safe except for a pony, its shafts still fastened to a tub. If only someone had pulled the pin out of the shaft, the pony would have escaped and been saved, everyone said. Who is to say what they would do in a situation like that? I gave it a lot of thought as I imagined what it must have been like for the poor pony.

After leaving school, I became a full-time errand boy. I used to go to sleep with two phrases ringing in my ears, 'Look sharp back,' and 'when you've done that…'.

I wasn't thrilled with the job, but it was better than going down the pit. Really, I was playing for time, hoping to grow a little so that I could get a job on a farm.

Time seemed to be running out as I lay in bed one night. Ma and Father were arguing in the next room. I overheard him say, 'When I've kept a lad until he's fourteen, it's time he kept himself.'

Ma told him he'd not kept me a day since I was born, but I wasn't interested in her reply, I could only think of what he'd said. All next morning at work, I was still pondering over the problem.

Mr Surgey, the shopkeeper, gave me a box of groceries and said, 'I want you to deliver these on your way home for dinner. It's half past twelve, so you can go now.'

After delivering the groceries, I started to make my way home, when a bus pulled up to pick up a group of men. They were going to Langwith colliery. Impulsively, I jumped on the bus. Had I stopped to think about it I'd never have done it. The men told me I had to see Mr Meddlecot, the under-manager, if I wanted to work at the pit.

Mr Meddlecot looked at me dubiously when I asked if there were any vacancies. 'You're very small. Are you sure you're fourteen?' he asked.

'Well, I wouldn't be asking for a job if I wasn't.'

The impulsiveness was beginning to wear off. I'd have been relieved had he said no, but instead he asked when I wanted to start.

It was now or never. 'Tonight,' I said.

He looked surprised. 'It's your lucky day, the doctor's here this afternoon and if you pass the medical you can start.'

Later, I signed my name in a book and received two brass discs with a number engraved: one to exchange for a lamp and one for the banksman to allow me down the pit.

All afternoon I walked around the village, too scared to go home. In the evening, both tired and hungry, I went back to the pit and sat in the stables. At ten o'clock, I joined a queue of men at the lamp cabin, handed in my disc and received a lamp. The lamp was big and heavy, and when I carried it, it almost touched the ground. The lamp man, a bit of a wit, called after me, 'Shall I put a wheel on it?'

A long flight of wooden steps led up to the landing and the entrance to the cage. To me it was like going up to the gallows. A man behind me sensed my nervousness and asked if it was my first time. 'Yes,' I answered, 'and if I feel like this, it will be the last.'

Packed like sardines in the cage we waited for it to start. The cage lifted about a foot. Props removed with a bang. Then we were on the rope. Suddenly, the cage seemed to go from under my feet and we seemed to be falling at great speed. There was a flash of lights as we passed the other cage going up and a sudden jerk, as we seemed to stop dead. Then I felt as if we were on a yo-yo, bouncing up and down. A voice behind me said, 'Bloody fool, he thinks he's still winding coal not men.'

It was like entering another world. The lights were so dim and when I left the pit bottom there were no lights at all, only the one I carried. I followed a deputy who was carrying a battery, a length of cable and a stick like a scout pole. He used these to fire shots. All night we seemed to be walking or crawling; and at times into what appeared to be a rabbit hole. The deputy did quite a lot of grunting as he wriggled through; for the first time in my life, I was pleased I was small.

At two o'clock in the morning the deputy said, 'I think it's time we had our snap,' and he went to his coat, which was hanging up, and brought out a tin of sandwiches and a bottle of water.

I sat slightly to his rear; I didn't want him to know I'd nothing to eat. Much later, when he said it was time to make our way to the pit bottom I was falling asleep as I walked. I was almost too tired to be frightened.

The ride up the shaft was better than going down. The man behind me gave me a nudge to get off; I was almost asleep.

Now the hour of reckoning was coming. I sat on the bus going home, wondering what was going to happen. All my life my mother had made it clear, I wasn't going down the pit and now I had. I was too tired and dirty to do anything else but go home and face the music.

Ma sat in the rocking chair with a blanket round her. She had been there all night but she didn't sit long when I walked in. It was the biggest thrashing I'd ever had and yet after a night down the pit it didn't seem to matter. Then it was question time. Why had I done it; why had I not told her? What was the use, it was too late to explain. I slumped onto the rug in front of the fire; I was dead tired.

Ma grabbed me by the hair. 'Not in my house,' she said as she paraded me to the bathroom. 'Get yourself bathed and then I've something else to say to you.'

After a good bath, it all seemed like a bad dream, until my mother's voice seemed to bark at me. I expected her to say, 'All you have to look forward to down the pit is getting killed or maimed.'

I was wrong, instead she said, 'You've made your bed and you can lie on it, but remember my lad, the only way out of the pit is the army.' I never forgot those words and they came true.

In the pit bottom, there were three decks on the cage and the tubs of coal lowered from the top landing to the middle and bottom landing on a lift or hoist. The weight of the tubs of coal on one lift would pull the other lift up with empty tubs. My job was to collect the empty tubs as they came off the cage and push them round a passage and onto the lift. Then I had to help push the tubs of coal onto the cage. The target was one wind a minute and if you did anything to cause a delay, you were for it. There were two men and a boy on each deck. One man was the on-setter; he helped to push the tubs of coal onto the cage and rang a bell when he was ready for it to go. The other man pulled the tubs of coal off the lift and helped to push them onto the cage. It didn't improve my confidence when I found out I'd acquired the job through a fatal accident. A man had slipped and his foot had gone under the lift as it dropped down. He died later in hospital of lockjaw. It didn't take long for me to realise the key to the job was timing. Once the tubs were moving they didn't stop until they were on the lift.

The following Friday I drew my wage of twelve shillings and sixpence; with stoppages and bus fares that left ten shillings to take home. The scale of wages was two shillings and sixpence a day at fourteen years and three pence a day rise after three months.

Everyone was full of praise how a small boy had mastered such a hard job. The under-manager congratulated me one day, but a few minutes later, he gave me a clout on the ear. As he returned from inspecting the decks, one of the tubs I pushed had come off the rails. He asked what was wrong.

'I can't get this tub back on the rails.'

'There's no such thing as can't,' he said as he clipped me round the ear. 'Try, yes, but can't, never.' He lifted the tub with one hand and said, 'You see, I tried.'

The men were furious that he'd hit me. They thought I was barmy when I said I was pleased because he'd taught me a lesson.

Apart from my secret dread of the pit, I was quite happy at work and I was among some important men. Bernard Chambers, the on-setter on top deck, was one of the stalwarts of Mansfield Town Football Club, the 'Egg and Milk Team' who beat Walsall and just lost by one goal to Arsenal in the Cup.

Lol Taylor, the on-setter on bottom deck where I worked, was an all-round athlete and runner. He was my idol. He told me he trained on boiled tripe and onions, followed by a bottle of Guinness. Although I ate lots of eggs and milk, and a Friday night supper of boiled tripe and onions with a Guinness, my stature remained the same.

I could have cried one day when I came home from work and Ma told me we were moving house again, back to the street where we lived before in Clowne. The council house rent was too much for us, as we still had to repay the money for the strike food vouchers.

It was a very nice house and the rent was very reasonable. It belonged to the owner of a furnishing store. Ma had done a lot of cleaning and decorating for him. We never had a chance to appreciate the new house because Ma started to be ill before she could get it to her liking. She did her best, but I could see she was getting worse.

What started as a slight swelling in her feet had spread until her legs were twice the size; only willpower kept her going. Then she had a slight stroke. The doctor ordered her to bed and I stayed off work to look after her. Father explained if he stayed off work, it would give the manager an excuse to sack him. I could see the logic in that and I wondered if the same reason kept him going to the pub. Within days, my mother became almost helpless and I knew she wouldn't last much longer. She became distressed that I had to do everything for her. The following day Father told me to fetch Winnie.

First thing next morning I cycled the three miles to Whitwell. Winnie came straight back with me and it almost broke her heart when she saw the state Ma was in.

I couldn't believe it when my father suggested I should go to work that afternoon. I knew Ma had just a few hours to live.

'You can't do anything now and we shall need the money,' was all he said. He was right, I'd done everything and all I'd to do was say goodbye.

Her last words to me were, 'Colin, it's a hard world; look after yourself, and never give in.'

The afternoon was a nightmare; I couldn't keep my mind on my work. Lol Taylor suggested I went and lay on a bench and they would try to manage, but I had to keep going. We had just pushed the tubs of coal on the cage and as I turned away, everything went black. When I eventually came round, my workmates wanted me to go home, but it was an eight-mile journey and no buses until the pit bus at half past ten. Just before I fainted I'd looked at the watch, it was twenty past four. I knew there was nothing to go home for. Later on, Lol Taylor asked me what had caused me to faint like that.

'Haven't you had any dinner?' he asked concerned. He knew Ma was ill and thought I'd neglected my food.

He was surprised when I said, 'My mother's just died.'

'Do you mean before you came to work?'

'No, I just know she died at twenty past four.'

He couldn't understand it and neither could I. Later, I asked Winnie, and she confirmed it.

The next few days were full of arguments. All the family, including aunts and uncles, had to be invited to the funeral.

'Why?', I argued, 'where were they when they were needed?'

'It's the custom,' Father said, but he wanted to change the custom when I asked what I was going to wear.

When I started work, Ma bought me a second-hand suit in a green heather-mixture cloth. I said Ma might have come from an Irish family, but I wasn't wearing the green suit for her funeral; I'd go to work instead. At the last minute, Father bought me a second-hand navy-blue suit. Ma's wishes were no tears and no flowers, but we had the lot. The following day at work came as a relief. The men at work were so considerate; pieces of cake and pastries. In the end, I had to tell them, 'I've lost my mother, but I'm not starving.'

Ernest Ballinger was waiting for me one day as I jumped off the pit bus. He said he was sorry about Ma's death and that he'd been looking out for me during the past week.

'If I can help you in anyway, I will,' he said. He gave me a newspaper saying, 'I've marked an advertisement that may interest you. Think about it.'

Later that day I looked through the paper. He had pencilled round an advert: *Post offered to boy of good character, aged 14 to 16 years to train in gentleman's service.*

This could get me out of the pit and more importantly, get me away from home. I sat down, wrote a letter and then started building castles in the sky. I quickly had a reply thanking me for my application and a request for me to send three suitable references and then they would be prepared to offer me the post.

I had a reference from the vicar, the manager of the Cooperative store and a very good reference from the colliery manager. I sent all three with a letter, feeling confident I'd get the job. About a week later, I had a reply; my hands were shaking as I opened the envelope.

It was very brief; my castles fell as I read: *Dear Sir, I am sorry to inform you that we cannot consider anyone for this post who has worked in a coalmine.*

Ma's words came back to me, 'There's only one way out of the pit my lad and that's the army.'

Christmas arrived and passed unnoticed that year. I hadn't the heart to go carol singing. I'd not been to church since Ma died. My thoughts became bitter as I thought of God. Who's God? His face didn't shine further than the first three rows in church and it certainly didn't shine down the pit.

Calamity seemed to strike at work too. Halfway through the shift a man came to tell me the pit-bottom corporal wanted to see me on top deck and take my clothes with me. That meant a fresh job and I wondered what it could be. As I reached the top of the steps on top deck a lad passed me, a man had his arm round his shoulder. I thought he was ill until I saw his hand, dripping blood and with his finger ends hanging off. The blood seemed to drain out of my body, not with the sight of his hand, but the thought of the new job.

There was a haulage rope made of steel wire running overhead and the tubs fastened to the rope by the means of a chain.

'Come here,' said the corporal, 'I'll show you how to go on. Here's a chain with a hook at either end. Put one hook in the coupling of the tub, and then throw the other hook over the rope three times, catching it each time so you have three loose laps with the rope running through them. Hold the laps slack until you've got three, then drop the chain across the hook and let it tighten up.'

It sounded simple and looked simple when he did it, but I had two questions.

'How did the other lad trap his fingers and why have you picked me?'

'He used his fingers to hold the laps, instead of the flat of his hand. I've picked you because I think you have more sense than that, so let's see what you can do.'

Following his instructions, it was reasonably easy. With practice, it became easier and I realised that was the danger because complacency set in. There was no chance of me doing that, for every time I put a chain on, I thought of mangled fingers. My fear wasn't a fear of physical pain, but fear of being maimed, and as my father had been, thrown on the scrap heap.

After a few months of this, I decided to leave Langwith pit and find work at Cresswell; it was four miles nearer home and within cycling distance. There was a drawback, but I hoped to get round that.

After the 1926 strike everyone at the Cresswell and Bolsover pits received leaving notices and then signed on again, with one condition: that they joined Spencer's Union, which was the coal owner's sponsored union. I didn't want to join the coal owner's union so when I filled in my application form to sign on at Cresswell, I left the space blank where it asked that question.

When I handed the form back to the clerk he said, 'I expect the chief clerk will notice the omission, but if he doesn't, fair enough.'

The work was entirely different at Cresswell. On the first shift, after showing me how to harness a pony, I then took it to the levels near the coalface. The corporal on the level was a kind sort of fellow. He showed me how to put the shafts on the pony and fasten them to the tubs and then he took me to the coalface. My job was to take empty tubs to the coalface and bring full ones out, but that was only part of the job, as I soon found out. We almost reached the coalface when the rails seemed to disappear under water. I shone my light and there was water as far as I could see.

'This is a water stall,' he said, 'but it's a short one in advance of the others, to take the water.'

This water had to be hand pumped into tubs and taken out like the coal. I never dreamt I'd work up to the waist in water, but there I was. The corporal was sorry he couldn't give me another job, but this was the job allocated and he couldn't change it. He advised me to bring a spare pair of short pants, so that I'd have dry clothes to go home. Very soon, I was helping to fill water barrels as well as taking the tubs in and out. Paid so much a barrel, the men could earn more filling water than coal. They gave me five shillings every Friday for helping them. Out of my wage, I bought carrots, and every day there was a carrot for the grey pony. His name was Twig, the fastest pony in the pit.

During the week, the ponies had their stable near to where I worked, but at the end of the last shift of the week, they had to go to the pit bottom, which was four miles away. It was like the 'Charge of the Light Brigade' as some lads sat astride their ponies and had a race to the pit bottom. Two things put me off riding. In places, the roof was so low, that the only way of not getting scalped, was by lying flat on the pony's back. From time to time, the under-manager waited with a bucket of whitewash and a brush. If he saw anyone riding, he splashed them, and if any whitewash were on the rider or pony when they arrived at the stables, there would be a deduction of five shillings from their pay.

Every Easter bank holiday, the pit-ponies came from their home underground to the surface, where they were rode in pit-pony races. Bookmakers were laying odds and some of the lads made a bit of pin money giving the bookmakers an idea what the ponies could do.

I went to the races, not with the idea of making a fortune, for I only had a shilling in my pocket, but because I wanted to see Twig run and also I had a carrot for him. He was in the third race and as soon as the betting started he was 'odds on'. I went down to have a look at him and he recognized me at once and started nibbling around my pocket.

'Is this your pony?' the hostler asked.

'Yes, but the lad on the other shift is riding him,' I replied.

'No he's not, he's ill, so get the bridle on him, it's time you were at the start.' I tried to think of an excuse, but the hostler cut me short. 'Come on, they're waiting for you.' He grabbed my leg and threw me on the pony's back. All I could hear as I lined up was the cry, 'Six to four on Twig.'

'My God,' I thought, 'I mustn't fall off.'

The starter dropped his flag and I clung on for dear life, because Twig didn't have a saddle. As I neared the winning post, a roar went up from the crowd. Twig nearly slipped as he swerved to the right, while I carried straight on. I sat up on the ground with all the stuffing knocked out of me, but I was soon on my feet and running, as a crowd of angry men, who had lost their bet, advanced towards me.

A few weeks later, I had my first accident in the pit. It happened while taking the ponies to the temporary stables at the end of the shift. We walked two abreast when suddenly a lad dashed in between us with his pony. This particular pony had a habit of lashing out if anything touched its back. The lad walking alongside me slapped the pony on its back as it passed and up went its heels. My last recollections were of two horseshoes flashing under my chin. The next thing I knew, I was being carried as if a baby in a man's arms. As my senses returned, I recognised the man carrying me was Alan Dobbs.

At the ambulance room on the pit top, the deep cut to my jaw was cleaned and dressed. Suddenly Allan Dobbs jumped out of his seat as the ambulance man fetched the tweezers to pull out some of my teeth that seemed to be hanging out.

'Don't you touch those, just put a bandage on, the rest is a doctor's job,' he said and he took me home on the bus.

I couldn't eat or drink, so I just waited until the evening to attend the local doctor's surgery. By the time I arrived at Chesterfield hospital, it was late at night. I had a broken jaw and stitches to the lacerations on my face. Next day I arrived home with a contraption like a crash helmet around my head and face, and a cup with a spout, so that I could feed myself with fluids.

Imagine my surprise when after only one week, the compensation doctor summoned me to the colliery. 'Start work in seven days,' he said without even examining my jaw.

'But I haven't had anything to eat for a week,' I protested.

'Get some bread and milk down you,' he replied.

What else could I expect, he wasn't paid to administer medical justice; he was paid to save the coal owner's money. It was another three weeks before I started work and even then, I couldn't eat solid food, but we had to have money to live.

The water in the section where I worked was always deepest on Monday morning having collected over the weekend. To make matters worse, the sole came off my boot and although I tied it up with string, the pebbles found a way through. With a sore foot and no prospects of getting any new boots after four weeks off work, I wasn't in a very good mood.

As I passed the colliery office on my way to the cycle shed at the end of the shift, a thought flashed through my mind. I'd go and see the manager and if he couldn't solve my financial problem then he could find someone else to paddle through the water.

I never realised how difficult it was to see a manager. The clerk had a dozen excuses why I couldn't see him. He wanted to know what I wanted, but I knew if I told him, then my chances of seeing the manager were nil.

After I'd waited half an hour the clerk said, 'It's no use waiting, you won't see the manager today.' This made me more resolved.

'If I've to wait two and a half hours until he comes out then I shall see him and if not, I'll go and knock on his door at home.'

The clerk went into the manager's office and a few minutes later, he called me in. Luther Henton sat at his desk. I could read his thoughts, 'What does this little shrimp mean by insisting on seeing me?'

'You know I make a point of not seeing anyone unless they state their business first.'

'The clerk told me that, but I had to see you otherwise I can't come to work tomorrow.'

'What do you mean?' he asked.

I bent down and pulled the string tied around my boot and the sole fell on the floor. 'I've worn these boots for less than a month and the water I work in rots them. I can't afford any more.'

'Well, what do you expect me to do m' lad?' He called everyone m' lad.

'Buy me a pair of boots, so that I can come to work tomorrow.'

'Come m' lad. If I bought you a pair of boots, I'd have everybody wanting them.'

'Well, tell them they can have a pair of boots and my job working in the water.' I glanced at the clock. 'I've got to go home to Clowne and I haven't had my dinner yet and the shops close at six, so do I get the boots?'

He wrote a chit out: *Please pay bearer three shifts.* 'Take this to the cashier,' and as I reached the door he said, 'and don't come to me for the next pair.'

I went to the shop for a pair of boots before I went home. I had a sense of satisfaction, not merely because I had the boots, but because I had the courage to go and ask for them.

Father never seemed settled in the house in Clowne, but I was surprised when he told me we were going back to Stanfree. I suppose I could have tried to get work at Oxcroft, but my childhood memories still prevailed. My thoughts turned in another direction. Why not get out of the pit altogether?

One Saturday morning I cycled to Mansfield and enlisted in the navy as a boy. There was a snag. One of my parents should have accompanied me, so I had to take a form of consent home for Father to sign. To make sure he didn't refuse, I didn't ask him. Instead, I traced his signature off the rent book. I posted it on the Wednesday, so that the earliest reply would be Saturday, when I'd make sure to meet the postman. I waited the whole of the following week. It was Thursday when I received a reply, with a travel warrant, to report to Mansfield the following Monday. I hid the letter under the linoleum floor covering in the bedroom.

Once again, my luck ran out, when on Saturday morning Erma kicked the chamber pot over. During the mopping up operation, the letter and warrant came to light. I could never understand why my father wouldn't let me go. My argument, that if I went as a boy I'd learn a trade, seemed to fall on deaf ears and on Monday morning, we both went to Mansfield.

The recruiting officer smiled when he saw us, thinking Father had come to see me off. His smile vanished when he heard what had happened. He promptly fetched another form for Father to sign but he still refused despite threats of forgery charges. The next day I was back at the pit. This seemed destined to be my lot. Instead of sailing on the water, I must paddle through it.

A few weeks later, something happened that I'd been dreading ever since I started at Cresswell. Twice a day during the day shift, I took an extra empty tub as far as some air doors. Once there, I helped a man push it through the doors onto the airway, where he was keeping the way clear, and we then collected the full tub and pushed it out. To me this was the worst part of my job as tobacco juice soon covered my arms because as we pushed the tub, the man kept spitting his tobacco juice, like bullets out of a machine gun, over my hands and arms. It was ironical, he was the union secretary and I was the only one not in the union.

One particular day he said, 'I've noticed you don't pay your union dues.'

'What are you going to do about it?' I asked.

'You can't work here unless you are in the union.'

'So I look like leaving then.'

'I hope not,' he said and then went on to tell me all the benefits. He lost his temper when I pointed out that a vicar couldn't serve both the Lord and the Devil and neither could his union serve the coal owners and the workmen.

'You've got until Friday to make your mind up,' he snapped.

I made up my mind before mentioning it to my father. I told him I had to join Spencer's Union or finish.

'You wouldn't join it if your mother was here, but I'll leave it to you,' he said.

My God, I thought, why didn't you leave it to me when I wanted to join the navy?

The next day I went to work with mixed feelings, but my feelings had a change for the worse about mid-morning, when one of the tubs came off the rails in the water. I asked one of the men to give me a lift with the tub. At that moment, they were doing a job they couldn't leave, and so they asked me to do what I could until they could help me. After a lot of frustration and with the help of a batten and pieces of wood as fulcrum, I managed to get the tub onto the rails, but by that time, dirty slimy water covered me.

The straw that broke the camel's back was when a voice shouted, 'Put those battens across the water, so that we can get across.' It was the manager with some visitors. I'd just been wallowing in it, now they wanted me to make a bridge for them.

'You can paddle through it like I have to,' I shouted and stood there while they rolled their trousers above their knees and waded through the water.

When the manager reached me he said, 'Get your clothes m' lad, and get off home.'

'That's fair enough,' I replied, as I picked up my clothes and started to walk away.

'Take this pony with you,' he shouted.

'You take him, I've finished,' I answered.

Later that day I had to see the manager to fetch my insurance cards. I had a surprise when he said, 'You've lost a day's pay now m' lad, so let that be a lesson, and you can come to work in the morning.'

'No, I never believe in turning back, so you had better give me my cards,' I replied.

The most obvious place to get a job was Oxcroft colliery as it was on the doorstep. So overcoming my childhood fears, I went for a job. The pit was strange, but I knew everybody who worked there; I'd grown up with them. I set out to show them I could work and they were quick to praise me, yet they always coupled it with my father. 'You're a worker like your dad.' What short memories they had; hadn't they called me Ballinger when I was a child?

A new concept was coming into the mines. The haulage ropes extended right to the coalface when previously they only went as far as the levels. Instead of taking the tubs onto the coalface, conveyor belts and shaker pans took the coal to a loading point. The changes brought a sharp increase in accidents. An old man, Albert Dawson, was one of the first. He had his arm amputated between wooden supports and a shaker pan. My job, although harder, was more pleasant than wading through the water at Cresswell, but somehow I couldn't settle. Sooner or later, I had to get out of the pit. I realised what Ma meant when she said, 'Men's backs are cheaper than supports.'

On my seventeenth birthday, I thought of my life up to that moment in time: a daily walk, eight hours down the pit, then bed; another day gone. A trip to the cinema in the cheapest seats and a weekly instalment on a gramophone saw the end of my pocket money. I'd seen the sea once in my life: a day trip to Cleethorpes with the Apple Tree Inn children's outing. Ma's words came back to me again, 'There's only one way out of the pit.' So once again, I was looking for the recruiting office, but this time it was to a room at the Three Feathers Inn, Chesterfield.

The Reluctant Soldier

T he recruiting sergeant looked doubtfully at me as I stood under the measuring board and then on the scales.

'You're half an inch too short and three pounds underweight,' he said. 'But don't despair, try again later.'

I made a regular pilgrimage to the Three Feathers after that, but my body just refused to expand.

One weekend Father asked me to cycle to Worksop on an errand. There was an army recruiting office and I called in. The result was the same, underweight and under-height.

'What kind of scholar are you?' the sergeant asked.

'Average, I think. Why do you ask?'

'Well, there's a special enlistment for the Lincolnshire Regiment. You can get in underweight and -height if you can pass the education test. Do you want to try?'

I'd not visualised going into the infantry, but thought I might as well try. I completed the test: just a few easy sums, a short essay on why I wanted to join the army and some general knowledge questions. The required age to enlist was eighteen years old, so I lied and added a year to my age. 'You'll hear the result in a few days time and then you'll have to attend here to be sworn in.'

I enlisted on 23rd April, St George's Day, 1931. It seemed such a serious business, with my hand on the Bible. I'd hoped to return home in time to go to work on the afternoon shift but when handed a shilling and told, 'You're now a soldier in His Majesty's Army and must not work in civil employment,' my hopes were dashed.

There was a confrontation with my father when I returned home, but this time he couldn't do much about it, apart from try to get my discharge on the grounds of underage.

Waiting for Monday morning seemed like waiting for a new life to begin. As I travelled by train from Clowne to Lincoln, the last pit I passed was near Worksop. I vowed that I'd never go down a pit again, and thanked heaven there were no pits in Lincolnshire to remind me.

At the barracks, a friendly corporal greeted me and showed me the barrack room, dormitory and canteen. There were already about fourteen lads all in civilian clothes. Apparently a few days elapsed before the issue of uniforms. The corporal explained we were just killing time until there were thirty of us, and then we would start the sixteen-week training course. He also added that if any of us wished to go out from four o'clock to half past nine, we could.

Some of the lads were getting ready to go out, so I decided to go out as well. I didn't join the others, but followed on behind. When I reached the gates, they were in the guardroom, where a corporal was writing their names in a book.

'Right off you go and be back by half past nine,' he said, and then he turned to me. 'Where do you think you are going?'

'Out,' I said.

'What else?'

This didn't make sense to me. 'What do you mean?' I asked, 'I was told I was allowed out, and you've just let those others go.'

His face went red and he bellowed, 'When I ask you a question, you call me Corporal, now get off back to your barrack room.'

Back in the barrack room, I was smarting under the injustice of it, when a couple of lads said that the corporal was out of order and not allowed to do that.

'Look,' I said, 'I am not interested in what he's allowed to do, just tell me if there's another way out of this place?'

'You can get over the latrine wall,' one of them said, 'but you have to be a good climber.'

I managed to get over the wall and thought I'd a good prospect of getting back, so off I went to the cinema in Lincoln.

Later, I managed to scramble back over the wall, and as I was getting into bed, the door opened and a huge man stood in the doorway. 'Don't get in there boy,' he shouted, 'I've got a bed for you,' and he marched me to the guardroom. What a start to my new life.

I didn't sleep a wink, so the bugler next morning wasn't needed. The same huge man who had taken me to the guardroom was behind me as I marched into the office to see the commanding officer. Perhaps I wasn't going up the steps fast enough. I felt a hand grasp the top of my trousers, and when my feet touched the ground, I was standing in front of the CO's table.

He read from the paper in front of him, 'Absent from roll call, breaking barracks and damaging the latrine wall. Well, Marshall, what have you to say?'

The chap who helped me up the stairs seemed intent on helping me to get my words out. He kept prodding me in the back with his stick.

'How do you expect me to say anything while he's poking me in the back with a stick?'

'Stand away from him Quartermaster Sergeant. Now look here Marshall, the way you are acting you are not going to be accepted into this regiment.' Then in a fatherly voice he said, 'I'm not going to spoil your crime-sheet; as a matter of fact you don't have one yet. I'm going to let you off this time, and I want you to realise the responsibility of joining such a famous regiment. Marshall, do you still wish to become a soldier of the Lincolnshire Regiment?'

I couldn't believe my ears, I thought I'd been in the army for days, but now in view of the events of the past twenty-four hours there was doubt in my mind. 'No Sir, I've changed my mind.'

The CO bounced his fist on the table, 'Damn me man, it's too late!'

I couldn't help but say, 'Why did you ask me then?'

'March him away, and don't let me see him again,' he shouted in exasperation.

Nothing seemed to make sense anymore. Allowed out, and then you're not. You're in the army, and then you're not. They ask if you still want to join and when you say no, they say it is too late.

Barrack room inspection, endless parades but after tea was the worst part of the day. Blanking equipment and cleaning brasses I could hold my own with any of them, but when it came to the chin-strap, bayonet, scabbard and boots, it was soul-destroying to me. The first night I sat with the bone handle of an old toothbrush, a mug of water and a tin of polish, rubbing away for hours on end. That was the last time, because after that I'd stand on parade and there would be twenty-nine pairs of toecaps shining like mirrors and mine.

'What filthy boots! What do you mean by it?'

'They're clean Sir. But just clean.'

There was no question of boning my boots after that because I never had the time. I hadn't finished one lot of defaulters before I started another, which meant extra work from five o'clock to seven o'clock. I was a fool to myself really, but I just couldn't resist answering back.

On one occasion, the sergeant major called me to him as we left the parade ground. 'Marshall, I'll make you sorry you ever joined this regiment before I've finished with you.'

'If you remember Sir, I was sorry the day after I came here.' To me, a statement of fact, but the charge was 'insolence'.

The squad sergeant seemed to have been checking my habits, for one day he came to me and inquired, 'Why is it you are first on parade for PT, school and even dental checks, yet you are last for everything else?'

'They're the things that are most important to me, and I've satisfaction doing them,' I replied.

One thing I really enjoyed was the hour in the gymnasium. I could have stayed all day. I felt as fit as a fiddle and it showed on the progress report. The rest of my report wasn't so flattering.

One thing I didn't have any interest in was Regimental History. One day when I wasn't paying attention to the lesson the instructor asked me, 'Marshall, what is the most outstanding thing in the history of this regiment?'

The answer came without having to think, '"…and they sustained heavy casualties." It's on almost every page.' Then I added what was on my mind, 'How can you have heavy casualties and call it a victory? It reminds me of the coalmines, where they only count profits and not the losses in life and limb.'

Poor man, his heart and soul were in the regiment. I felt I'd stepped on holy ground. I was soon on familiar ground, as I was marched with an escort to the guardroom. The provost sergeant came into the cell. He was curious to know what had happened. 'You've been placed under close arrest on a serious charge. What have you been doing?' When I told him, he laughed. 'Old Challis takes his schooling too seriously, but I wouldn't like to be in your shoes tomorrow.'

The CO was in a very understanding mood. He blamed my youth and upbringing, another reflection on my working-class background. I had a feeling he was trying to play the whole thing down. 'I shall regard this as insolence, and you'll be confined to barracks for seven days and let that be a lesson. You could be on a more serious charge.'

On the fourteenth week of basic training, we took our third-class certificate of education. I achieved top marks for Regimental History, which proved my point. I knew it, but didn't agree with it.

The weekly rate of pay was fourteen shillings, but all we drew was five shillings, the remainder left in credit. Most of the lads were hard up, and quite a few were in debt to a fellow who lent them money. He was a newsagent who had a pass to come into barracks with newspapers, and on the side sold cigarettes and chocolate. An obliging sort of chap, he lent money to buy his commodities, with interest at twenty-five percent per week. It wasn't long before some of the lads owed their wages even before they were due. Being continually on defaulters, I couldn't go out or even have time to spend my money in the canteen.

Near the end of our basic training, we took the second-class certificate of education exam. I was anxious to pass as this meant an increase of three pence per day in pay.

It was the last day of training when the results came through. I'd passed, so although still confined to barracks, it brightened up what looked like being a dismal weekend.

The rest of the squad were going on draft leave. Some of the lads were moaning that they wouldn't be able to go on leave because they owed the newsagent moneylender so much money. These lads had been bled white for weeks. Admittedly it was their fault, but I felt sickened at the way this corruption flourished.

I saw the adjutant walking to his office. Without a second thought, I dashed across the square, gave him a salute and asked if I could speak to him. 'This is highly irregular Marshall. What do you want?'

I asked him if he was aware what was going on with the money lending business. He was surprised to hear about it and promised to deal with it first thing next day. 'Why not deal with it now, so those lads can go on leave in the morning?' I asked.

'What's the bee in your bonnet Marshall? How do you propose I should deal with it now?'

'You could cancel the newsagent's pass into barracks until later tomorrow, then he can whistle for his money until they come back off leave.'

He slapped his cane against his riding boot, 'Jolly good idea.' Then he walked off chuckling at the thought. He turned his head and called to me, 'By the way, you'll be going on leave as well tomorrow.'

It was my first leave, but the lads I knew at the pit had neither the money nor the time to go out during the week. I remembered one of the lads in my squad called Jack North from Pleasley. I looked him up, found he was having the same problem, and he invited me to spend the rest of my leave with him and his parents.

On the last day at the Lincoln Depot, we marched in to see the CO one by one. As I stood there, my mind went back to the day eighteen weeks before when he asked if I still wanted to be a soldier, and my answer was still the same. The moment I went in the office, I thought I was in for another lecture. The CO was rummaging through a heap of papers.

'What a collection,' he said as he looked through my crime-sheets. 'If it was anyone else I'd be recommending them for discharge.'

'And why not me, Sir?'

'Well, I've checked with all the instructors, and they all say the same thing. On odd occasions, you've shown you are as good as the best. It's not that you can't do it, but you've deliberately set out not to do it. You came into the army on the wrong foot and I am going to give you a chance to change step. In my report, I've recommended you for promotion to the Signals. For God's sake make an effort.'

As the train moved off I thought, that's the last time I'll see Lincoln. Many thoughts had been passing through my mind. The CO was probably right and a career in the army was better than the pit. I made up my mind to have a go.

Our battalion were looking forward to going to Pembroke; the advanced luggage had already gone as we boarded the train. Looking out of the window as we passed Reading, I could tell by the sun we were still travelling north. Turning to the others in the compartment, I asked, 'Anyone want a bet we're not going to Pembroke?' What a pity I only had two pounds; I could have made a fortune. For some reason, there had been a last minute switch. We passed through Grantham before they conceded I'd won my bet, and after buying tea and cakes all round, I wasn't much in pocket. We reached our destination at last, Catterick Camp, North Yorkshire. A Scottish regiment had gone to Pembroke instead, the decision not made until after our advance baggage had already left for that destination.

Apart from the YMCA, there were no social activities. The nearest town was Darlington, about twelve miles away. It didn't worry me whether I served my time in Catterick or Timbuktu, so long as it was soon over, but when winter came, I began to long for the South.

Spring came at long last and with three years' service, this made me the princely sum of three shillings a day.

One day during that summer Lieutenant Bill Hastie, the Signals Officer, asked if I'd like a tour of duty at the Lincoln Depot.

'A tour of duty doing spud peeling and cleaning lavatories? No thank you,' I replied.

'They wouldn't ask HQ Company, if they wanted a spud peeler. Actually, they want a clerk, but also someone who can turn his hand to anything. I thought it would be an opportunity for you. You can do anything but be a good soldier.'

I left Catterick knowing that I'd never meet a fairer officer than Bill Hastie. As I went through the barrack gates at Lincoln, I thought perhaps it would be different this time.

After the first week, I'd settled down in my job. I'd a pass to wear civilian clothes and bought a smart suit. All I was short of was my freedom. There was a lot at stake now. If I got into trouble, I forfeited my civilian pass for three months, and I was due for a month's leave in August.

I felt great going on leave in civvies. To be able to blend with the crowd, even in the local pub I felt at ease the first night I went out. I met Joe, an old school friend, for a drink. He suggested I join him for a weekend to Glossop, near Manchester, where he was courting a girl called Esther. She had a cousin named Phyllis and we could make a foursome. I'd never bothered with girls before, and I wouldn't take a girl out while I was in uniform. I told him I'd stay Saturday night and then catch the train for Sheffield next day.

What a night Saturday turned out to be. Phyllis was a very quiet girl, but behind the quietness, there was a sense of humour.

I wanted to go to the Speedway at Bellevue, but the others preferred the local cinema. Phyllis pushed in front of me at the box office. 'I always pay for myself,' she said, 'and by the way, I'm a speedway fan too, but I can't afford it.'

The film was interesting until I noticed a smell of something burning. I saw a wisp of smoke rising and looked down. My trouser bottoms were smouldering. The man on my left jumped up and made for the exit, he'd dropped a cigarette end in the turn-up of my trouser leg. By the time I snuffed it out, there was a burn hole right through. I played it down a bit; at that age you like to impress people. Inwardly, I was fuming. I didn't smoke, yet a clumsy clot had burned a hole in my only suit.

I walked home with Phyllis, and when we reached the top of her street, she said she would rather go down the street by herself. It seemed the proper thing to do was to kiss her goodnight, but obviously, it wasn't. It was like putting a match to dynamite. She struck me across the face with her half clenched hand. I felt her nails in my cheek and with a kick on the shinbone, she flounced off.

When I reached Esther's house, Joe and Esther were very concerned about the scratches on my cheek. I said the first thing that came into my head – I'd slipped and brushed my cheek against a hawthorn hedge at the top of the street. Thankfully, there were no more questions until Esther went to bed.

'Now tell me what really happened,' said Joe.

'I've had my trousers burned, my cheek gashed, my shin bruised, all because you brought me here to take a wildcat out.'

Next morning I started to dress and found the trousers to my suit were missing. I put on my spare pair of flannels and went downstairs. Apparently Phyllis had fetched my damaged trousers to repair, and I'd get them back after dinner. Personally, I wasn't bothered about seeing her again, but since she had my trousers, I'd no option. After dinner, Joe and Esther went out for a walk. Her father was sleeping in the armchair and her mother had gone to lie down on the bed. Phyllis came in with the trousers under her arm.

'Here you are: duly repaired and pressed,' she said, as she dropped them on my knee. I must have been staring at her so intently she blushed and said, 'Aren't you going to inspect them?'

I looked at them, she'd made a marvellous job and I thanked her, but my mind wasn't on the trousers. What a gentle face she had. Could this be the wild cat from last night?

'When are you going back?' she asked and we both burst out laughing. I'd explained to her the night before that when a soldier goes on leave, the first question everyone asks is, 'When are you going back?'

'Aren't you going to walk home with me?' she asked.

I put a hand to my cheek.

'Sorry I can't repair that,' she said.

As I walked her home, she apologised for the previous night. She'd heard so many adverse stories about soldiers and when I kissed her, she'd panicked. I arranged to meet her again and when I took her home that night, her mother suggested I could spend the rest of the week with them.

Phyllis worked in a paper mill, but she also had to help at home. The holiday couldn't last forever, but after my leave ended, I was counting the days to the next. Every other weekend I was on my way to Glossop. In between there was a stream of letters; a new dimension seemed to have come into my life. This went on until the middle of November, when I fell foul of the red tape again.

Walking down the main drive on my way to the main stores for the monthly supply of stationery for the office, a car whizzed past me from the rear. I recognised Lieutenant Wilson. When I reached the main store, a police sergeant followed me and told me I was on a charge for not saluting an officer.

'You must be joking,' I said. 'He flew past me from behind.'

'I'm not joking, I've been told to put you on a charge, as you deliberately turned your head away as the officer drove by,' he replied.

I wasn't especially worried when I went before the company commander next morning. How could they expect me to salute an officer coming from behind at about twenty-five miles per hour, even though there was a ten-mile per hour speed limit in barracks? However, you cannot argue with the establishment.

If Lieutenant Wilson said I turned my head away he must be right, he's an officer and they don't know how to tell lies and as for speeding? A load of rubbish, Lieutenant Wilson wouldn't go down the main drive as fast as that.

'Seven days confined to barracks and you can forfeit your next weekend leave. March him out Sergeant Major.'

Of all the punishments I'd had, this was the most unjust, all for not having eyes in the back of my head.

As I walked away, I heard the sound of a motor approaching from behind. I knew it was the milk lorry, but I gave it a smart salute. The sergeant major's voice drowned the sound of the engine as he called me back and marched me back into the office. 'Are you trying to be funny, Marshall?' he asked.

'No Sir, just playing safe. If I'm to be punished for not saluting an officer coming from behind in a car, in future I may look stupid, but I'll be safe.'

I believe in the end they regretted giving me those seven days punishment. I never missed a salute after that; it became a standing joke.

I had to write a letter to Phyllis explaining my detention on BTDs (bloody tedious duties) and so I couldn't see her that weekend. The next letter I received caused me a little concern. She had been to a church concert with George. She'd mentioned George once before. He was an assistant to the vicar, a proper gentleman. When she wrote later saying George was becoming a regular visitor, the alarm bells started ringing. Pass or no pass, I was going to Glossop. On the Saturday, I missed my dinner so I could catch a train to Manchester. Phyllis was surprised when I walked in, especially as I was wearing uniform.

'Why didn't you let me know you were coming?' she asked. That annoyed me. She could have said, 'When are you going back?' and we could have laughed it off.

'Have you made arrangements to go out?' I asked.

She looked embarrassed as she replied, 'Yes.'

'With George?' I knew it was a foregone conclusion, but I had to know.

'Yes with George. What are you going to do?' She was getting worried now.

'I could spoil the appearance of the proper gentleman, but I won't. I've enough sense to know a dog at home is better than two are away, so I'll catch the next train back to Lincoln. I'm supposed to be in by midnight as I haven't got a pass.'

'Will you get into trouble?' she inquired with some concern.

'Not if I'm in by midnight, and if I'm not, it doesn't matter now. For the last four months, I've been walking a tight rope trying to keep out of trouble, so that I could come and see you. Now, suddenly it doesn't matter anymore.'

I missed the train from Manchester by about five minutes, so I walked down to the first hotel to get a drink. Four youths were at the next table and when one of them spoke to me, I was rather apprehensive; soldiers and civvies didn't mix too well in those days. They asked me to join them and when I did, they all drank up.

'What's the idea?' I asked, 'You ask me to join you and then you drink up as if you're leaving.'

'We're going on a pub-crawl, one drink in each pub in Oldham Road. Are you coming?' they asked.

Only a fool would go on a pub-crawl on an empty stomach, but then only a fool would let gentleman George take his girl without putting up a fight. I'd no idea where Oldham Road was, but my new acquaintants were well briefed, and in no time, we were having a drink. As I went to sit down one of them said, 'We'll not be here long enough to sit down.'

I lost count of how many pubs we went in. Sometimes the voices and bright lights were near; sometimes they seemed miles away. The last thing I remember was a tramcar passing with its bell clanging. I was on my own. Had I come out of the pub without them? I couldn't remember. All I knew was that I had to sleep.

Someone shaking me brought me back to my senses. Daylight was streaming through the barred window high up the wall. The scene was familiar, but the place was strange.

'Where am I?' I asked the man who was holding a mug of tea.

'Drink this,' he said, 'we'll ask the questions.'

With a head like mine, I didn't need questions. As I spent the day sleeping off my hangover, I reflected ruefully on the previous night. The police filled in the blanks. Apparently, I was flat out on the tramlines and all I could say was, 'Let me get some sleep.'

On Monday morning, after a fine of two pounds ten shillings, I was on my way back to Lincoln. When I reached the barracks the sergeant on the gate greeted me with a chuckle. 'You're in for it this time, my lad,' he said.

The CO had a buff envelope on the desk in front of him from the police. The charges were, absent without leave for forty-two hours and being drunk in a public place. What did I have to say?

'On the charge of being absent, I make no excuse. I went to Manchester on personal business and I didn't get back. I accept your punishment for that.'

He thumped his fist on the buff envelope. 'What about this lot? Getting drunk and acting like a fool?'

'I don't have to answer that charge Sir,' and his face went crimson.

'What are you talking about?' he demanded.

'I went before a magistrate yesterday and was fined two pounds with costs, so the army authorities don't have to deal with that because under Military Law you can't be punished twice for the same crime.'

'Eight days confined to barracks. March him out,' he barked.

What a chorus in the barrack room when I walked in, 'We all thought you were going to the glasshouse at Aldershot!'

Confined to barracks didn't matter now. I didn't care if I never went out again; my life seemed empty. There would be no cross-country runs and no voluntary PT. I hadn't the heart to do anything. I knew it was best to forget Phyllis, but I couldn't. Burning old letters didn't help; I could remember all that was in them. The Christmas present I'd bought her lay in my locker. I didn't know what to do with it. I felt I couldn't give it to anyone else. We had joked about it for so long, after she scratched my face on the first night we met. I said I'd buy her a manicure set, so I sent it, with a very short note saying: *There are no strings to this, but I just couldn't give it to anyone else.*

At Christmas, although due ten days' leave, I only stayed for five. Drinking seemed to be my only interest, and I didn't find much pleasure in that. This was the beginning of the worst part of my service. I seemed hell-bent on getting into trouble.

One day, when marched in to see the company commander, I knew the papers on the desk were mine because I was so used to reading my name upside down.

'What now,' I thought, 'back to Catterick?'

'You came here as a utility man Marshall. Well, can you cook?' For once, I was lost for words; the last thing

I wanted to be was a cook. 'The cook for the sergeant's mess is going into hospital, and you have been recommended to fill the gap.'

This was a challenge. My mother had taught me to cook, but that was for four of us. The company commander stopped tapping his pen on the desk. He was waiting for an answer. I felt like asking a lot of questions, but he would think I was hedging.

'Alright, I'll have a try.' At least I'd have no more barrack room bull.

I shared a bunk in the sergeant's mess with the waiter. He was a chap I already knew from the gymnastic team and we became the best of friends. We had two different temperaments; I was outspoken and impulsive and he was cool and calculating. He would readily tell you his name, 'Smudger Smith', and jokingly spell it for you – 'S M I double F', but beyond that he played his cards close to his chest. I gathered he was a bit tight for money, and concluded he must be making a big allowance to his parents.

The first time Smudger was on church parade, he came into the kitchen wearing his uniform. It was so threadbare, I rolled over with laughter. 'How long have you had that?' I asked.

'About four years. Anyway, what's wrong with it?'

'Come on Smudger, you haven't worn that suit for a long time, have you? What's the set up?'

'Well the cook, Jimmy Borringer and I were never on parade at the same time, so we pooled our kit. This is Jimmy's suit and belt and my boots, bayonet and cap. That's the set up.'

I looked at the clock, 'You'd better be quick and put my suit on or they'll say I'm a bad influence on you.'

We formed a marvellous relationship at work and socially. There was no question of who did what. The steward said the job had never gone so smoothly. Smudger never mentioned girls when we went out. It was straight to the bar. I knew why I wasn't bothered about them, but I couldn't make him out at all. As we sat having a drink one night he said, 'I was wondering about something. If you could get your civvies out of the stores, I could go out of the back gate.'

'What makes you so interested in my civvies all of a sudden?' I asked.

'I'm getting engaged on Saturday and I thought...'

I cut him short. 'Look Smudger, if you've any designs on my suit, you'd better put your cards on the table.'

I was a lot wiser when he'd finished. He'd not been making an allowance to his parents, but to a girl. This was the only way he could save. She was working, and between them they had a nice little nest egg and planned to marry later in the year.

'What about the suit? I suppose you want to borrow it for the engagement, and hope I give it to you for a wedding present. Is that right?'

'No, only half right,' he said, 'lend me your suit for the engagement, and I'll buy a new one for the wedding.'

An epidemic of diphtheria put a stop to Christmas leave that year, as we were all isolated. Smudger was one of the first to catch it, and he was so bad I didn't think he would survive, but his physical fitness pulled him through. This was the first Christmas I'd spent in barracks.

It was coming round to the King's birthday parade. Smudger and I still had only one good kit between us, so it would be rather awkward if we were both on parade together. This had never happened until the week before the actual birthday parade. A few of us had a shock when we read the detail for the following day: *General Attendance and No Exemptions*.

Some of the men hadn't been on a parade ground for two years. Smudger fetched his suit and looked at it ruefully. 'Do you think I'd get away with it?' he asked.

'Well, if you could get away with that you may as well have my boots and bayonet. You can only go inside once.' I pulled a coin out of my pocket and said, 'The one who wins goes on parade, the loser goes sick.'

Smudger called, I spun the coin and lost. Next morning I told the orderly corporal to put me on a sick report. He went up the wall.

'Look at this lot, more than half the depot on a sick report.'

He'd just begun to call me all sorts of horrible names when the door opened, and the sergeant major popped his head inside, 'Sick parade straight after breakfast and General Attendance put back until after sick parade, Corporal.'

This is going to be interesting, I thought, as we marched to the medical room. My name was at the bottom of the list, so whatever symptoms I had, would have to be played out before I went in. I sat near the door of the consulting room. It was hilarious to listen to the different complaints: headaches, backaches and stomach aches, some couldn't go to the toilet and some couldn't stop. The MO seemed to have a general cure for everyone – medicine and duty, which meant going on parade. When my turn came, I knew it was no good making some lame excuse. I thought I'd appeal to his sense of humour, if he had one.

'Well Marshall, and what are you suffering from?' I was hoping for that sarcastic introduction.

'There's nothing wrong with me Sir, I feel fine. It's my bayonet that's bad.'

He slapped the table with his hand. 'Damn me, you're the only man who's come in here this morning and told the truth.' The smile left his face and he suddenly looked serious as he asked, 'Is it very bad Marshall?'

'It's the worst I've ever seen. It's so bad, it's green.'

'You're excused all duties with the privilege of getting into bed if you feel like it. I also suggest you get some methylated spirits, a bone and a burnisher on that bayonet to make it better.'

I never mentioned our conversation, but it went round barracks like wild fire.

I began to look forward to Christmas because I met a fellow called Wilf Cheetham, who I knew from my school days at Shuttlewood.

Wilf was a big strong chap, although only nineteen years old he was a charge man on the coalface at Oxcroft. We struck up a friendship because we seemed to be the only ones in the village with any money to spend on going out. When on leave, Wilf would often ask me to go with him to see his mother. He would also say, 'Our Nancy's home on holiday,' but I'd never been with him.

On Boxing Day 1935, we went to see two local teams play football. On the way back, we passed his home and he suggested calling in. He introduced me to his sister, Nancy. She was sitting on an old-fashioned sofa that had seen better days, but she looked lovely enough to be sitting on a throne. I couldn't follow the conversation; I just couldn't take my eyes off her. It wasn't until we were walking home that Wilf said, 'We're making a foursome at a dance tonight. You and Nancy are joining me and Hettie.' This was my introduction to the girl I married.

Nancy had left home and gone into service at the Warehousemen and Clerks' School at Cheadlehulme near Manchester. Our courtship was difficult in the extreme. We were both tied, Nancy to the school and me to the army. We wrote to each other every day, and I made sure she wasn't short of postage stamps because all I had to look forward to were her letters.

Nancy's time off work consisted of: one half day per week and one day off per month, plus a few days during school holidays when she went home.

The army began to seem more and more like a prison. I was just counting days, and then hours and in the end seconds. My tour of duty at Lincoln eventually ended. I didn't apply for an extension as most of the men did.

I arrived back at Catterick just in time to see the battalion march out *en route* for Malta. Trouble was flaring up in Palestine and the brigade on standby. There was about twenty of us left behind; a skeleton staff.

The battalion eventually returned from Malta, and it was back to the old bull and whitewash. Life became humdrum, except for the day when we had to land a boat near Redcar. We were the 'invading force', and as the boat neared the shore, a man stood up ready to jump out. He was carrying a Lewis gun and as the boat beached, he lost his balance and fell overboard. The cry went up, 'Grab that man.'

The officer's voice boomed out, 'Grab the gun; bugger the man.'

He has the makings of a coal owner, I thought, as my mind went back to the days in the pit.

At the end of the exercise, I had another reminder of the pit, but in a different way. The CO gave it out that anyone who had made friends with the local community, and if they were invited, could stay the weekend with them. Word must have travelled round and quite a lot of my company had invitations. I wasn't expecting one because I hadn't got beyond passing the time of day with anyone, so it was a surprise when a chap came up to me.

His speech and dress was a good match. Check cap, white muffler round his neck and a whippet at his heels. In a broad Durham accent he asked if I'd like to stay with him and his wife, and added, 'Ah've nowt, but tha's welcome to it.' He told me his address, 'Silver Street, Cowden' and I promised to go there for the weekend.

Brought up in a mining community, I'd seen my share of poverty, but nothing like that house. The floors and table were bare, but scrubbed as white as snow. The stairs and bedroom were the same. The man's wife, Peggy showed me where I was to sleep. By the way of an apology she said, 'It's only a straw mattress, it might not be very comfortable, but it's clean.'

I found out she was right on both counts. My first meal was toast and pork dripping. Jack, my benefactor, jokingly remarked, 'You'll get a fair share of this over the weekend, the boss buys the pig and we buy the sweat from it.'

Saturday dinner was a concoction I'd never heard of before, one of their specialities; it looked horrible, but tasted good.

'Don't expect anything else until supper. Daisy there was catching your supper before daylight this morning,' Jack said.

Coming home from the local pub that night, Jack stopped and put his hand on my shoulder, 'Our Peg's a good cook. I can smell the food from here.'

It smelt delicious as Peggy started to serve the rabbit stew. Jack fetched a dish from the shelf, 'Here you are Daisy. We don't forget who caught the rabbit.'

It was no wonder that dog never left his heels. Sunday dinner, the rabbit stew was finished off with vegetables from the garden. I really enjoyed that meal, so I insisted on helping to wash up, much to Jack's disapproval.

When I left that afternoon I felt so indebted to them, I put my hand in my pocket, I knew I'd about ten shillings over after my fare back to Catterick. Jack pushed my hand down in my pocket saying, 'We don't take payment for nowt. You were welcome to share it.'

It was at Christmas that year that Nancy and I became engaged. There was no hope of us getting married until I'd left the army and found a job, but it was nice to know she was prepared to wait.

Christmas over and I'd three months left to serve. I hadn't a lot to show for my seven years. I was a bit bigger, a lot stronger and had more confidence. At last 22nd March 1938 arrived, the day of days. When I returned my kit to the store, I felt a tinge of regret when handing in my bayonet; perhaps the next owner would polish it beyond recognition. The CO shook me warmly by the hand and wished me luck. I went to draw my pay, and as I saluted the officer, it passed through my mind that I'd have to work for my next pay, but thank God, I wouldn't have to salute for it.

Looking For Work

Day in, day out, within a twelve-mile radius of my sister Winnie's home I looked for work. All I heard was, 'We'll bear you in mind,' but never, 'start tomorrow.'

I decided for the time being, I'd have to go back to the pit. I'd spent a month looking for work, and now I had to have a job or sign on the dole.

The following Monday morning I started work at Markham Colliery near Bolsover. I worked in the Black Shale, which was the deepest of three seams worked at Markham; the other two were the Deep Hards and the Eli Coal.

It was a frightening experience, the first day on the coalface. I'd never seen anything like it. Instead of the roof being flat, here and there were rolls of black shiny rock. Some were so low you could just wriggle underneath. It was a work of art trying to put timber up to the roof to support it. The work didn't frighten me; it was all the warnings. Everyone I saw said, 'Watch that, don't go under there and beware of this.' At the end of the shift, the deputy came and asked if I'd been all right. He laughed when I told him I'd had so many public warnings, I ought to be disqualified. I'd known him since my school days in Stanfree. He said, 'All the men know you've just come out of the army, and they don't want anything to happen to you.'

On my second week at Markham, the deputy told me that I had to go on the night shift the following week because the order was: last to start had to go on nights.

I wasn't going on the night shift for two reasons. Firstly I wouldn't be able to go to see Nancy, who was now working for a manufacturing chemist named Daniels and his wife at Duffield, and secondly, I'd been perturbed by the conversation I'd heard between the men during the past week. There seemed a general opinion that the Black Shale would 'go up' one of these days. I started to wonder if it was just pit talk, just something to say, until I met an elderly man who had been working in the pit for years.

'You know Colin,' he said, 'we shall wake up one morning and find the Shale gone up in smoke.'

'What makes you so sure of that?' I queried.

'There's as much gas in that gate as there is at Bolsover Gas Works and all it wants is something to set it off.'

'If it's as bad as that it could go up anytime,' I said.

'You're right, it could, but they fire shots in the 'ripping' on nights, and I wouldn't be down the pit then, for a pig and nine young 'uns.'

I cycled home from work on Friday afternoon and I caught up with a railway man pushing his cycle up Bolsover hill. I jumped off my cycle and walked with him. In conversation, I asked if there were any jobs going on the railway, and he told me about a new Goods Yard at Derby.

Next morning, long before the offices opened at Derby, I was waiting for the manager to arrive.

If I could get a job, I wanted to be back at Markham pit to pick up my cards as the office closed at noon. How I was going to get them was another problem.

When the manager asked about my experience and qualifications I told him I had four qualifications: intelligent, fit, strong and willing. He laughed and asked if I was working at present. I lied and told him I'd just come out of the army. As I'd been talking, he'd been writing on a form and he passed it to me. 'Start work here, next week.'

The under-manager at Markham was surprised when I went to see him and asked for my cards. 'Is this because you've got to work nights?' he asked.

'Partly, but I'm not cut out for pit work.' I didn't want to prolong the interview, the insurance clerk would be going home very soon, and I wanted my cards before he left.

'I'm afraid I can't give you your cards immediately, you'll have to serve your notice to leave.' His tone sounded very uncompromising.

I knew the army was my only hope of getting my cards, so looking very serious I explained. 'I've been to Worksop and rejoined the army this morning, and I go back on Monday morning.'

He wrote on a slip of paper and said, 'Take this and fetch your cards before they close.' He stood up and offered me his hand, wishing me the best of luck.

I felt a cheat. The only consolation was there would be a job for some poor soul who stood outside his office the following week.

Returning to Winnie's that night, I thought I ought to go and see my father. I'd not seen him since I came out of the army, and now he was in a wheelchair. As I walked from the bus stop to my father's house in Stanfree, I saw a man coming towards me, weaving from side to side. I gathered he'd been to the Apple Tree Inn, as he staggered into me. It was Dent Whelpdale, a neighbour of my father. Dent was a miner at Markham and he worked in the Black Shale, but he was on the night shift, one of the team of rippers. He put his hand on my shoulder, partly to steady himself. He was a fine built man over six feet tall. 'Colin, I know I'm drunk, but I know what I'm saying. This is the last time I'll ever get drunk. The Shale will go up this week, as sure as I'm drunk tonight.'

It seemed incredible, a man forecasting his own doom, and yet accepting it. Poverty seemed to have conditioned him into that state of mind. I shall never forget Dent Whelpdale, or his last words to me. As I put my head on the pillow that night, I felt lucky to be out of it.

Early on Monday morning, I went to Derby with my belongings in a suitcase. After signing on at my new job, I left my case at the station and went in search of lodgings. They weren't difficult to find, but suitable ones seemed to be very scarce. However, a friendly police constable recommended a place.

The family consisted of Mr and Mrs Smith; they were pensioners, with a daughter at home named Flora, who was about four years my senior. The old man was willing to take me in the moment he knew I'd been in the army. He'd been a sergeant major during the Boer War, and if his wife hadn't interrupted him, Mafeking would have been relieved again. She was a calculating woman; she needed the money, but not me. She hurried to explain it wasn't personal, but her daughter was engaged to a young man, who was upper-middle-class and he might think it degrading taking in a lodger. It was Flora who broke the deadlock.

'Don't make that an excuse Mother; you know we aren't officially engaged. Take the gentleman in. I can't see what difference it would make.'

Over a cup of tea, we discussed terms. Mrs Smith left me in no doubt, she wanted as much as she could possibly get. I knew what to expect to pay, but she quoted quite a bit more. However, it was a spotlessly clean and comfortable bungalow. We agreed on terms, and straight away, she wanted paying in advance. Mrs Smith was a hard nut, but I'd no objection. I reminded her if I paid in advance, I could leave without notice. The moment I paid her, she started to read the riot act. When I came home from work, she would expect me to take off my overalls and wash before sitting down at the table. No smoking in the bedroom. Be in no later than eleven o'clock. Ask if I wanted the radio on. Don't leave dirty washing about. She would have gone on had I not interrupted her by reminding her that she could always ask me to leave. After unpacking, I had a walk to clear my head, somehow I felt like a heap of manure in a rose garden, needed but not welcome. As I walked, I pondered about the prospect of my new home. I began to regret my decision to stay there. Suddenly I became aware of the time and had to run to get back so I wouldn't be late for tea. It reminded me of running back to barracks. Perhaps I'd have to ask Mrs Smith for a late pass.

During the meal, Flora sensed I wasn't feeling at home, and suggested that if I wanted to stay in, she would lend me a book to read. She pointed to the bookcase saying, 'Those on the left are mine, help yourself,' and with a glance at her mother added, 'I wouldn't bother with the others.'

Settling in the easy chair with a book, I decided it wasn't too bad a place after all, so peaceful. However, it wasn't to be. Poor old Mr Smith couldn't miss the opportunity to brief me on the Boer War and the Relief of Mafeking. He must have worn himself out talking to me, because about nine o'clock he announced he was turning in. When he'd gone to bed, Flora said, 'He's not a bad old chap. He may have been a sergeant major in the army, but he doesn't have much authority here.'

As I prepared to go to bed, I suddenly remembered I didn't have an alarm clock and I asked Flora if they had one I could borrow.

'Don't worry,' she said, 'Father will wake you and your breakfast will be on the table by the time you are washed.'

As I ate my breakfast next morning, I could have echoed what Flora said: he wasn't a bad old chap.

There were about thirty men standing outside the converted railway carriage, which served as a site office. Another one nearby served as a cabin for the men to sit at break-times.

One of the men came up to me; obviously, he could see I was a stranger. 'Take your mashing can to the cabin and Old Fred will mash ready for your break.'

'I didn't know you had mashing cans, I'm not used to this work yet. I'll get one for tomorrow.'

'Look out for me at break-time, you can share mine.'

As the foreman dispersed everyone to various jobs, he said, 'Do you know the fellow who called to you when you arrived here?'

'No, I don't know anyone this side of Chesterfield.'

'Well he's Sid Walker. I'll put you to work with him digging foundations, but don't kill yourself trying to keep up with him; he's one of those keep fit addicts.'

During the first break when I was sharing the contents of Sid Walker's mashing can, the foreman said, 'Did you say you came from near Chesterfield?'

'Yes, why do you ask?'

'One of the drivers has just told me there's been an explosion at Markham pit, and I wondered if you had any relations working there.'

I felt numb as I said, 'I've no relations, but I've friends.'

My thoughts went to Dent Whelpdale. I hoped his prediction hadn't come true. It all depended at what time the explosion happened. There were three pits at Markham, it could have been any one of them, but I knew it was the Black Shale.

When I went back to my lodgings for dinner, I could hardly eat for the questions Mrs Smith kept firing at me. Was it a deep pit? Do you think they would get the miners out? What a difference a tragedy like this could make. Today she was all over me, yesterday, hardly a word. When I stood up from the table, leaving half of my dinner, she looked surprised.

'I thought you had an hour for dinner?'

'I do,' I replied, 'but today there are a few things I must do. Also I want to call to buy a mashing can.'

'No need to buy one, you can borrow my husband's, he won't use it again.' She fetched a blue enamelled can with a lid from the cupboard. I offered to pay her for it. 'No, you can use it while you are here.'

On the way home from work I bought an evening paper. It didn't give much definite news. The explosion had happened at the end of the night shift. I started to think of the men I knew who would have been there. Every member of the Smith family bought a newspaper; four newspapers in one house, such was the interest. To them it was a strange tragedy, to me it was different; they were men I knew.

When I met Nancy that night the subject came up repeatedly. What would have happened if I hadn't left the pit? I believe the death toll was ninety-eight men, and there was to be a thorough inquiry. I wondered how thorough it would be.

I'd settled down to my job, also, Mrs Smith was much more amiable. It was my second week in Derby and I was feeling happy. I went home for dinner one day to find a red-faced Mrs Smith dashing around the kitchen, and a pile of cakes and pastries on the table.

'You'll have to hurry up with your dinner, I want to get the pots washed quickly,' she said.

'Is there anything wrong?' I inquired.

'No,' she snapped, 'Gerald is coming for tea, and I want everything ready.'

I bit my tongue. I felt like saying, 'You won't get Gerald to the altar by baking, you'll need a shot-gun for that.' I must admit I was curiously looking forward to teatime and meeting Gerald of the upper-middle-class.

After work that day, I took off my overalls, had a good wash and since we had a visitor, I changed my clothes. I was going in for tea when Mrs Smith met me in the hall, she pointed to the kitchen. I popped my head round the door and there was my tea on the kitchen table, neatly laid out on a tray. I picked up the tray and walked into the dining room. Their faces reminded me of the time I dropped my rifle on ceremonial parade.

'You'll have to excuse me Gerald,' I said, 'but I'm not used to eating in the kitchen. In my home you can't get in the kitchen for wet pit clothes.'

Flora recovered her composure and introduced us, and then tea went on thankfully as normal.

Gerald's parents owned a large drapery store in Derby and he was the manager. He had a car and a houseboat on the river. He suggested Nancy and I could make a foursome with them one weekend, but I took that with a pinch of salt. Later on, Gerald took Flora out in his car. The old man was in the kitchen with a pile of dirty pots. I helped to dry them.

'I didn't know you were on defaulters, Pop,' I joked.

'Don't know about defaulters, but I wouldn't like to be in your shoes,' he said.

I heard Mrs Smith banging things about in the next room. 'Do you think that's the war drums beating?' I asked.

When Flora came home, the first thing she asked was, 'Did Mother play hell with you?'

'No,' I said, 'as a matter of fact I haven't seen her since tea. She did quite a lot of banging while I was helping your father with the washing up.'

'It took the wind out of her sails the way you talked to Gerald. He talked more last night than I've ever known him. I don't know why,' she said puzzled.

Although I was risking alienating her, I had to tell her. 'Flora, the poor man can't be natural with two worshipers round him, like you and your mother. You treat him as if he was a god. As things are, I can't see him ever marrying you. Can you?'

Her lips quivered as she replied, 'No I can't, but what can I do, give him an ultimatum?'

'There's no need to do that. Just stop spending the weekend on his boat until he announces your engagement, or he finishes with you.' I doubted she would take my advice, but I felt better for telling her.

Mrs Smith adopted a standoffish attitude, but I wasn't bothered. The old man and Flora were both amiable, I was happy at work but then the inevitable happened.

I'd been to see Nancy, and the bus back to my lodgings was a few minutes late. It was ten minutes past eleven and the bungalow was in darkness. I rang the bell and the old man came and opened the door, grumbling to himself about being disturbed. Putting the light on in the kitchen, I started to make a hot drink before going to bed. I'd noticed Flora's bedroom door was open. She had a key, and her parents never knew when she came home. The old man stormed into the kitchen. I thought he'd gone mad.

'Don't you know that it's lights out at ten thirty? Put that light out,' he shouted at the top of his voice.

I couldn't stand anymore, 'Listen you old fool, I've put up with reveilles and lights out for seven years, but now it's over, so go back to bed and dream of your days of glory.'

Poor chap; I'm sure he was in such a state because of his wife buzzing him.

There was no call next morning; just a slice of bread and jam was all I managed for breakfast. The following morning Flora called me, and I made my own breakfast. Friday was the last straw, no breakfast and ten minutes late for work.

Sid Walker asked what was going on, and when I told him he said, 'I'll take you round to my mother's house and she may take you in.'

His mother was an elderly lady with a heart of gold. Her husband was a retired railway man and not in good health. She had a blind son and a young granddaughter living with her, yet I had to insist on giving her more for my board than she asked.

I told Mrs Smith that I was leaving after dinner on Saturday. She didn't answer me.

Flora said, 'I'm sorry you're going, but I don't blame you.'

When the time came, I started to pack my case. Mrs Smith came in and said, 'You are not leaving like this. I want a week's notice or a week's board.'

I reminded her that I'd paid in advance and was giving her the benefit of two days' board. I packed my case, and was on the point of leaving when she confronted me.

'If you leave this house, I'll send for the police. You've taken something that doesn't belong to you.' I tipped the contents of the case on the floor.

'If there is anything of yours, take it,' I said.

'Oh, it's not in there, you know where it is.'

My God, the mystery deepens, I thought as I started to repack my case.

'If you leave this house, I'll send for the police and tell them you've stolen my husband's mashing can.'

'That's ridiculous, you lent me the can and it's at work. I'll bring it back on Monday.'

She was adamant, 'Leave this house before you bring that can back, and I'll send for the police.'

The can wasn't worth much, but I remembered a lad at school who got three years' borstal for stealing sixpence. I offered to pay for it, but she refused. There was only one thing for it. I'd have to break into the cabin at work and steal the mashing can, which I'd already supposedly stolen.

I remembered as I went to the site that one of the windows had a piece of cardboard in place of glass, so it would be easy to get in the cabin, but I had to watch out for the railway police, for to get caught would mean losing my job. I fetched the can without incident and put it on the kitchen table, and left without a word.

I found a vast difference when lodging with Mrs Walker. The house was on John Street, a side street near the Midland Station. A long row of terraced houses lined either side of the street. The toilet was outside, and the bathroom was in the shape of a zinc bath hung on the wall outside. It reminded me so much of my childhood in Stanfree. At Mrs Walker's the reception was very different. No restrictions, just, 'Make yourself at home; I'll treat you like one of my boys.' She did ask me to do one thing, 'Put everything back in its place. My son is blind and he depends on everything being in its place.'

The food was plain, but good. She was a person who could make a meal out of next to nothing but what I appreciated most was her cheerfulness, she always greeted me with a smile, and God knows she had little to make her smile.

Her son George attended the School for the Blind, and in his spare time made cane chairs, shopping baskets and many other things. I marvelled at the way he cut the canes with a razor sharp knife and never cut himself.

The project for the new building at the Derby Goods Yard was nearing completion, and by the end of October, my work was finished. Nancy was very disappointed because after all the years we'd been apart, it had been lovely to see each other regularly. In addition, she knew if I couldn't find another job I'd go back to the pit as I wouldn't go on the dole.

Mrs Walker cried when I told her; she was such a soft-hearted woman. I told her I'd spend the rest of the week looking for a job, and if I wasn't successful, I'd go back home. She told me not to worry about my board, just give her what I could afford, but I wasn't prepared to add my burden to hers.

I went to stay with my sister Winnie and on Monday morning went once more to Markham for a job, but this time to the Deep Hards.

I met someone coming out of the offices and asked him if the manager was around.

'He's down the pit. I'm the Chief Clerk, what do you want?' he asked.

'I'm looking for a job.'

'Are you any good at sport?'

'Yes.'

'Can you run?'

'Yes.'

'Can you play football?'

'Yes.'

'That'll do, come into my office.'

After all the formalities he told me to start on Wednesday.

'What am I going to do? You haven't asked about my capabilities apart from sport.'

'Alright, I'll put you in the picture,' he said. 'You know there are three collieries in the Markham Group, us, Warsop Colliery and Markham Main at Doncaster. There's a lot of competition between us in the sporting field, and we always seem to lose out. This year we're going to change that.'

I came away rather bewildered. For the first time I'd been given a job on my sporting record.

During the first three days, I was with a corporal, who was in charge of the men and boys working in the pit bottom. He was also the trouble-shooter; if anything went wrong, he'd to put it right. His job was also to keep the coal coming out of the pit, or explain why. On the Friday, the under-manager inquired how I was getting on.

'He's doing fine, he can get about a lot quicker than I can,' the corporal said.

'Well, Colin, that's your job on Monday morning; let's see what you can make of it.'

'I don't want to take someone else's job,' I answered.

'It's alright, he's asked to come off it; he wants something steadier. He's getting too long in the tooth and stiff in the joints.'

It was spring 1939; I'd been out of the army for almost a year, and my worldly wealth totalled twenty-three pounds. It was hard going trying to save with paying my board, two journeys to Derby to see Nancy, the theatre or cinema once a week, so this didn't leave much over. Nancy and I talked things over, and decided our only hope was to get married. Perhaps it would be easier to save without the expense of commuting to see each other. The following week I took the tenancy of a house in Stanfree and found a woman to do the decorating. I had my army reserve pay and we used that to pay a local furniture store to furnish our home.

We were married on the 3rd June 1939 at Chesterfield register office. We would have preferred a church wedding, but we had to be realistic with the funds we had. Our honeymoon was a trip to Sheffield where we went on the market and bought a tea service for twelve shillings and sixpence. It wasn't much of a wedding, but the days and weeks after made up for it. For the first time in my life, I felt completely happy. I had the girl I loved and a home of my own.

War

There was just one cloud on the horizon, the talk of war. Although Chamberlain had been to Munich, the threat remained. It was August and already they had called up some reserves. My call-up papers came during the last week of August, and I had to report to Lincoln on Saturday 2nd September. What a week we had, trying to enjoy what could be our last week together.

A friend of Wilf, my brother-in-law, offered to take me to Lincoln. We arrived at the barracks about midday and they seemed to be bursting at the seams. Some faces and names I recognised at once, others left me searching my memory. Everywhere there was a queue. It took me over two hours to hand in my papers, and then I went in search of something to eat before I joined the next queue. The cookhouse had run out of food and I had no better luck at the canteen. Reluctantly, I joined the queue for my kit; this tailed off down the main drive and halfway round the football pitch.

It was so easy to send out thousands of call-up papers, but a normal regimental depot couldn't cope with such an intake as this. No wonder the sergeant major was exasperated when I asked him if there was any hope of something to eat and where was I going to sleep. He turned on me and for a moment, I thought he'd find me accommodation in the guardroom.

'You'll just have to wait. Can't you see we're doing what we can?'

I didn't want to harass the poor chap anymore, so I told him I knew where there was food and a bed and if prospects didn't improve, I'd be on the six o'clock train back home.

He shrugged his shoulders, as if to say 'What's one in this multitude?'.

When I asked the policeman on the gate if we were allowed out, understandably his reply was, 'You must be joking. Imagine what Lincoln would be like tomorrow if we let you lot out.'

History seemed to be repeating itself, I thought as I clambered over the latrine wall and made for the station.

The door was locked and the house in darkness when I reached home. Fortunately, I knew how to get in, and Nancy came home just as I was finishing a meal.

She was amazed to see me. 'What's happened?' she asked.

'They couldn't find me accommodation, so I've come home until they can.'

'Did they give you permission?' she asked anxiously.

'No, but don't worry, I told them I was going home.'

It meant a little longer together, but it also meant another tearful goodbye. I'd made a cup of tea and we lay in bed listening to the radio. We heard Chamberlain's speech at eleven o'clock and the declaration of war. That meant I'd to go back right away. There was no such thing as absent without leave in wartime; you were simply a deserter.

One of the neighbours took me on his motorbike to Worksop; from there I caught the train to Lincoln. Fortunately, this time the policeman on the gate didn't know me and I went straight to the guardroom. Instead of waiting for the sergeant to ask for my papers, I took the initiative: 'I should have reported yesterday, Sergeant, but I'd some trouble at home.'

'It's probably as well,' he said, 'we had more than enough here.' Without asking for my papers he said, 'You'd better report to the orderly room.'

There was still a queue at the stores waiting for kit, so I joined them. I hadn't a clue where to report, as I'd lost touch with events by going home. If I reported to the orderly room and told them I'd handed my call-up papers in yesterday, they would want to know where I'd been.

I saw Sergeant Major Garrett talking to a bunch of men on the parade ground, so I went up to them.

'Are you with this lot?' the sergeant major inquired.

'I don't know who I'm with to be honest; I've just drawn my kit, that's as far as I know.'

'Just stay here with me,' he said, 'when I get about fifty men I'll take you down to Stores Park. It's a good thing you didn't come yesterday; it was murder. Sergeant Clark didn't know if he was on his head or his heels, this place was bursting at the seams.'

'There doesn't seem to be many about today. Where have they gone?'

'We had to open up a disused garage at Stores Park. That's where you will be going in a short while.'

As we approached the dilapidated building, I thought it looked like an aeroplane hangar. Inside, laid out in rows were mattresses with blankets, just like hundreds of graves. When told to try to find a vacant place, I asked one or two men to put their beds closer and managed to squeeze in. I made sure I was near the door, because when I looked at the mass of straw beds, I wondered what would happen if a fire broke out. Of course there were plenty of 'no smoking' notices, but some people would smoke in a gas works.

Next morning after breakfast, we all paraded on the car park. There were too many of us to form up in any order, we just stood in a bunch.

The adjutant came on the scene, a sheet of papers in his hand. He stood on an old oil drum. 'Can you hear me at the back? I want to give everyone a fair chance,' he shouted.

He called for fifty volunteers for Blackpool. As they rushed forward, he gave the sheet to a sergeant, telling him to take the names and numbers of the first fifty. Then he called for a hundred volunteers for Brighton. There wasn't such a good response for Brighton. I think he realised it was too far away; he gave the sheet to another sergeant saying, 'Take the volunteers and detail the rest.' With a smile on his face he said, 'I suppose you'll all want this one: "A hundred for Scarborough."'

Once again, there was a scramble, and when the sergeant had filled the list and the disappointed ones turned away, the Adjutant spoke again.

'I've a little amendment to make to those three drafts; for Blackpool read Aldershot, for Brighton read Tidworth...' I never knew where the Scarborough draft went, it was drowned in the laughs of the crowd.

The rest of us were told to fall into three ranks. He walked down the ranks counting as he went. He counted fifty and put his hand out.

'From here to the right in threes, four paces to the right, march,' he shouted and turning to the sergeant major, 'That's the draft for Portland,' he said, and I was there.

It was with mixed feelings I joined up with the Lincolnshire Regiment again. I was pleased to see some familiar faces, especially the old signallers. We were welcomed at Portland by an officer, who told us the list of the overseas draft would be on detail the following day.

Next day you couldn't get near the detail board. There was a list of the whole battalion, company by company. When I eventually reached the board, and looked for my name, it wasn't there. I was feeling pleased with myself as I checked HQ Company, I'd a feeling I'd be in the Signals. No, my name wasn't there either. There was another sheet on the right of the board, it was headed: *The under mentioned are next for duty for the overseas draft*, and my name was on it.

A couple of days later, while waiting for the call-up, I received a telegram from Nancy saying: *Father, seriously ill.*

I was granted five days' leave and, as the battalion was due to sail to France the following day, told to report to the Lincoln Depot.

After five days at home, my father was out of danger, and I was back once more at the Depot. Most of the reserves had gone, and the men coming in now were Territorials. I'd just arrived there when Sergeant Major Garret arrived. 'Who can drive a car?' he shouted.

I put my hand up, knowing I was taking a chance on having to clean one.

'Right Marshall, report to the MO, you are his chauffeur from now on.'

As I made my way to the medical room I thought about my credentials; a crash course of a day in a Morris.

'Do you know how to get to Saxilby?' he asked.

'I can go by bus or train,' I was going to say, 'whichever is convenient.'

He cut me off saying, 'I don't care if you fly. Take this letter to the garage in Saxilby and bring my car back. Remember, I want to be in Sheffield this afternoon.'

I just managed to catch the bus to Saxilby as it was leaving. I gave the letter to the boss at the garage.

'There you are,' he said, 'it's ready.' He pointed to a blue car on the forecourt. I nearly had a fit. It was a Sunbeam Talbot: the car of my dreams. I trembled as I sat in front of the steering wheel. I'd never driven a car on my own. It took me a while trying to start it, then I put it into first gear and went very slowly onto the main road. I'll bet the garage man thought I was used to driving a hearse. After going up and down the gears a few times, I felt more confident and set off for the barracks. I knew a short cut instead of going through the city, and I was back in barracks in no time.

'How did it drive?' the MO asked.

All I could say was, 'Like a dream.'

'I'll not want you anymore today Marshall.' And that's how I became the MO's chauffeur.

One day after breakfast, Sergeant Major Garret came round with a sheet of paper in his hand. He wanted volunteers for a tunnelling company with the Engineers who were going to France. There were quite a lot of names on the sheet of foolscap, and without hesitating I impulsively said, 'Yes, I'll volunteer.' What an eventful week. My name was on orders transferring me to the Royal Engineers along with five more men. Draft leave was granted from Friday to Monday, when we were due to leave for Chatham. As far as we knew, we would be going straight from Chatham to France. It was a miserable weekend. It was hard to reconcile the love I had for Nancy with the fact that I'd volunteered to go to France, and might not be coming back.

What a surprise awaited us at Chatham. It was a deserted, damp and dirty barracks. About twenty soldiers arrived from different regiments, and all day others were arriving in small groups. There were no messing facilities, and we had to go to a neighbouring barracks for our meals.

Our first parade would have made a marvellous comedy. The Officer in Charge, Major Woods, called us to attention. He told us we'd be known as the 121st Tunnelling Company Royal Engineers, and he would expect us to maintain the tradition of the Royal Engineers. Then he gave the word of command, 'Slope arms!' About half of the men on parade started walking towards him, some saying, 'We do it like this Sir.' Others, 'We do it like that.' He turned to the sergeant, 'I'll leave you to sort this out,' and he marched off parade. Although there was some improvement by the end of the week, we still looked a ragged lot.

After a week of rumours, we learned we were going to France on the 13th January. There was no sign of mining equipment or transport, just an issue of small short-handled shovels for each man. The day before we were due to sail, two 30-hundredweight and a three-ton lorry with drivers, arrived from the Royal Army Service Corps Depot. At last, things were moving. The following afternoon we climbed into a lorry bound for Southampton. Under cover of darkness, we boarded the ship and the captain gave us a comforting talk before we sailed, reminding us of the enemy submarines and magnetic mines, and telling us whatever happened, we must not panic. We reached Le Havre without a single incident, but as we reached harbour, a seagull tried to dive-bomb us and collided with the radio mast.

What a welcome we had, as we loitered around the quayside. I felt like an undertaker at a wedding. Major Wood had a first-class row with a French officer, who seemed to be in charge of arrivals; actually, it was a second-class row via an interpreter. He had no knowledge of our arrival and the rations, which we should have for the journey inland, were not forthcoming. In the end, Major Wood ordered us to climb in the lorry and off we went; no one had a clue where.

Some four hours later, we passed a French barracks and they let us have some dry rations with a hot drink of cocoa, which I swore was diluted engine oil.

It was dusk when we pulled up in a little village miles from anywhere and I heard the CO shout, 'This is our destination.'

A crowd soon gathered round, no doubt the whole village. A man pushed his way forward to speak to the CO; he seemed to be the village representative.

One of my pals said, 'It's a pity he can't speak English, then we could understand what was going on.'

'I believe he only knows one word of French,' replied another. 'Everything the Major says, he replies, "*Non*".'

What a relief when a fellow who could understand a little French explained what was happening. The CO had asked if we could sleep in the village hall.

'*Non.*'

'Could we have a barn?'

'*Non.*'

'Could the villagers find us some food, and we would pay for it later?'

'*Non.*'

Red-faced the CO shouted something to the Frenchman, threw his arms in the air and walked away.

Apparently he'd given the village representative fifteen minutes to find somewhere for us to sleep and arrange some food. The villagers dispersed, but within minutes, they were back, bringing long sticks of bread with pats of butter and pans of hot milk.

It was a meal to remember: French bread, butter, and coffee made with milk. Later, a disused cottage was at our disposal with a few bales of straw. We bedded down in the four small rooms like cattle. The officers billeted at the nearby farmhouse.

Next morning, a lorry was sent to Abbeville to fetch some rations and utensils. Some of us made a makeshift fire-grate with some railings laid across a few bricks. The farmer let us have a few logs for the fire to cook, but not to heat the cottage. The CO advised us to keep moving about to keep warm, which was easier said than done. A fire was soon burning brightly; the shelves out of the cupboard were the first to go.

The next morning some of us went for a walk through the fields and came across a rabbit caught in a snare. As we carried it back to the cottage, wondering how we were going to cook it, a Frenchman from a neighbouring cottage dashed out and pointed to the rabbit saying, '*Lapin, lapin,*' and jabbering away in French, and pointing to his own house. We realised he was offering to cook it for us. We gesticulated there were eight of us, but he shook his head and put both hands up indicating ten. Ah well, we thought, he's counting himself and his wife, and we nodded in agreement.

Later that night he came to the cottage and beckoned us to follow him. Eight of us followed him to what we thought would be a lovely supper. There was a table with wooden forms placed on either side, ten steaming bowls of rabbit stew placed on the table, but in front of each bowl sat a little child. What could we say when those children looked as if they needed food far more than we did. The Frenchman seemed so proud as he took us to the adjoining room. There in a homemade bunk bed were four more little tots. He was equally proud of his sailor's uniform, although sent home, as the French navy didn't think it worthwhile keeping him in the navy because they would have to pay an allowance to his wife and fourteen children.

We had been in that God-forsaken place for a week. Most of the men had severe colds; I had a deep frost crack in my heel. There were no medical supplies. I began to wonder what we were doing there. Was a tunnelling company needed; or had we been sent out into the wilds to perish?

When I asked the CO how much longer we had to stay in those conditions, he said, 'You have to be patient and not question the wisdom of the higher command.'

'I'm not questioning anyone's wisdom Sir,' I said, 'but I thought you ought to know that everything burnable in the cottage has been burned, accept the outside doors and windows.'

I don't think he believed me, perhaps he thought we'd been running on the spot for the past week to keep warm.

We raided the farmer's stock of logs that night, and next morning the farmer, along with the CO, came looking for them. The CO almost threw a fit when he saw the cottage. Cupboards, doors and staircase had vanished; a rickety ladder was the only way upstairs.

'What's the meaning of this?' he demanded. I suppose he asked me because I'd approached him the previous day.

'You could put it down to survival.'

'I'll see you pay for this,' he said as he stormed out, the farmer trailing behind, the question of his logs forgotten.

Two days later, the CO came again, this time with two old ladies who owned the cottage. The damages they demanded, one would have thought we'd been billeted in a chateau instead of a cottage that had not been lived in for five years. The CO assured them he would pass their claim on to the authorities, and warned us we would foot the bill. We realised some good had come out of the incident when told we were moving out the following day.

One section stayed at Arras, together with the CO and his entourage. Another section went on towards the Belgian frontier; the other two sections went to Lens, a mining town in Northern France. I couldn't believe it at first, a mine without a slagheap, it didn't seem possible, but there it was in Lens.

We billeted in a dance hall in the main street. Two washbasins seemed inadequate, but it was two more than we had had at the cottage.

We were going to start work opening up the tunnels from the 1914-1918 war. When a draft arrived from England, it looked as though instead of being obsolete, we were going to have a useful purpose. I had a job the very first day.

A second lieutenant from Yorkshire had the job of surveyor. He came round looking for an assistant, but no one knew anything about the job. As a last resort, he asked if anyone had worked with the diallers in the pit. I'd worked odd shifts with them at Creswell, but that was all.

'Can you remember anything about it?'

'Not much, except for setting up the instruments. I don't know about the readings,' I replied.

'You set the instruments up, I'll do the readings, and we start after dinner,' he said.

From old drawings and plans, it was easy to find the first entrance to the tunnels. It was in a small hollow in the field about two hundred yards from the road just outside the town.

Opening that entrance was very difficult. Every inch had to be shuttered to keep the loose soil back. We studied the drawings; it was the Vermelles Sector. From where we were working there were twenty-two kilometres of tunnels or trenches as far as Vimy Ridge. Here and there, parts of the trenches remained, but the tunnel entrances had been filled in.

When the first entrance to the tunnel was opened, a skeleton of a soldier was found near the bottom; he must have been on his way up when the shell fell. The officer in charge of the surveying took a canary when we went in for the first time. It was like going back in time. There was hardly a stone out of place. The slogans on the wall were as plain as the day they had been written.

Another draft joined us from England, and we were split into three companies. This led to a lot of speculation that the Allies were planning tunnelling under the German lines. These speculations were cut short by a quick move to Doullens. HQ Company moved there from Arras and our two companies from Lens went to join them, for a rushed job making an underground General Head Quarters.

The site was an old fort, overlooking the town. The plans were to drift down thirty feet, and then open out with offices to keep the authorities safe and comfortable, with two brand new compressors. The job was soon underway, in fact, everything became more organised and men started going on leave. We even had an anti-aircraft squad, which I believe Major Thomson ran. We all knew him as 'Spit and Wink'. He'd been wounded and shell shocked in the 1914-1918 war, which left him with a mannerism that looked like a spit and a blink of the eyes, hence the nickname. He was a Canadian, and by far the best liked officer of them all.

I'd seen a lovely necklace in a shop in Doullens, a mother-of-pearl crucifix. After four weeks of scraping, I managed to save enough to buy it. If or when I went on leave, I wanted to take a gift for Nancy. Somehow, I wasn't an optimist about getting leave. As the days went by I became more convinced, so I put the necklace in a small parcel and asked one of the fellows going on leave to post it for me in England. I made a bargain with him, a hundred cigarettes to post it, and two hundred when I received word it had arrived. Perhaps it was as well that I didn't smoke, for cigarettes could buy many favours.

Unexpectedly the order came to pack up. We were moving out as a precautionary measure. A small force of German troops had broken through our lines, but there was no need to panic, reinforcements would push them back. This didn't seem to ring true as we left Doullens. The roads were chock-a-block with refugees, and surprisingly some of them were wearing French uniforms.

We arrived at a chateau three kilometres from Boulogne, and ordered to pitch our bivouacs. What a fiasco. Very few of us knew how to make a bivouac out of two ground sheets; it was hours before everyone was fixed up.

The officers billeted in the chateau, with three companies in separate lines in the grounds. It was really like a large field sloping away from the chateau. The following day confusion reigned. 'Strike your bivouacs, we're moving out.' Then, 'Pitch them again, we're staying.' At the end of the day, they went up and down like clockwork.

That evening we had permission to go to Boulogne with orders to be back by nine o'clock. It was hardly worth going for such a short time. A Yorkshire lad from Leeds and me were anxious to find out what was happening, so we decided to go.

News in Boulogne was very conflicting. Some said troops were arriving from England and some said troops were leaving. The NAAFI had closed and all the staff was packing up. We inquired where we could buy a cup of tea, and they directed us to the Salvation Army. I asked one of the staff when they were leaving. She smiled and said, 'Not until you do my boy.'

On our way back to the camp, a car came round a corner and pulled up with a screech of brakes. A woman driver wound the window down, and shouted in perfect English, 'Am I on the right road for Boulogne?'

I assured her she was, and inquired if she was English. She gave a cynical laugh and replied, 'No! Worse luck, I'm French, and my countrymen are running away back there.'

She'd come from near the Belgian border, and just escaped ahead of the German tanks. As we bid her goodbye, she made a startling proposal.

'It's a matter of days before you'll be overrun by Germans. Why don't you come with me to the South of France? You can get to Gibraltar from there.'

With time to consider it, I might have gone. 'You'll regret it,' she called to us as she drove away. How right she was.

Next morning an unexpected visitor came on the scene. A German bomber came floating over the treetops, and gave us a burst of machine gun fire, as we dived for cover. He didn't drop a bomb; probably he thought a bedraggled lot like us wasn't worth one. I felt sorry for two young lads who had just taken some rubbish to dump in the latrine trench. At the sound of the firing, they dived in. Perhaps it was getting away from that smell that induced me to volunteer for a covering party on a mission to blow up a bridge.

A second lieutenant was in charge of the operation. He was the only one out of the three companies who knew anything about blowing up bridges. He gave us a briefing before we set off. The Germans were advancing too fast, and this bridge had to be destroyed. It was a job for the Field Company, but they were safe in England, so the job passed to amateurs.

There was another snag. Fifth columnists occupied it, and it was this information that caused confusion when we arrived. The officer took two men with him and walked the length of the bridge. There was no sign of fifth columnists; he was very puzzled, and decided to play safe and find out more, so we returned to camp. When the CO telephoned HQ to inform them the bridge wasn't occupied and to check whether it was the right one, the brigadier was annoyed.

'Get your men back there and blow it up,' he snapped. 'You'll soon see whether it's occupied or not.'

Back we went once again. The driver really put his foot down this time. He was supposed to have a governor on the motor, so that his speed was limited to 40 mph, but that obviously wasn't working. I looked at the boxes of explosives piled at the front of the lorry and thought, if we crashed with this lot on board there wouldn't be many large pieces.

As we neared the bridge, we could see a couple with a pram standing at the far end. There was no inspection this time.

'Unload that stuff and let's get it over with,' shouted the officer, and we were eager to oblige.

As soon as we started to unload, we came under fire. The couple with the pram had fired first, followed by someone to our left and right. The bullets had gone harmlessly over our heads, but it was obvious they could have mowed us down had they wished.

'Let's get out of here,' the officer shouted, and we piled back on the lorry as the driver turned round.

We had reached the open country and the driver had just put his foot down, when a tank came into view behind us. Our driver slowed down. Looking through the window at the back of the cab, I could see the tank in the middle of the road with his gun pointing towards us. Just as I thought our driver was going to stop, we were all thrown in a heap as he accelerated. Above the sound of confusion, you could hear the hedge tearing at the side of the lorry. We were almost out of range by the time they could fire at us, but by the scream I heard, I knew someone was unlucky. When they finally said who it was, my body went cold. I'm sure he was the best living lad on that lorry, but it had to be him. His name was Ginger Baguley, a lad from Shirebrook, and one of the soldiers who had volunteered from the Lincolnshire Regiment.

When we arrived back at the camp, the CO tried to contact HQ to report what had happened, but the line was dead. All next day we stayed there like lambs waiting for slaughter. In the afternoon, I knocked on the CO's door at the chateau and asked him whether we were going to run or fight. His non-committal attitude was aggravating as he said, 'We shall have to await events.'

The sound of gunfire grew closer and closer. A passing cyclist informed us that a German tank was a kilometre away. Dusk was falling when there was a loud explosion. I thought Gerry was opening up with his heavy artillery until I remembered the lorry with the explosives parked near the chateau. There was pandemonium for a few minutes as the companies started firing indiscriminately in panic. Gradually, it calmed down, and Captain Pickering led us to a wood about half a mile away. He told us he would have to go back and tend to the wounded and added, 'Don't leave here until I come back.'

Realising we had nothing to eat, I slipped back to the cookhouse but all I could find in the darkness was four loaves of bread and some tins of Maconochie soup. As I fumbled around, I found a boning knife. I wrapped my handkerchief round the blade and put it in down my shirtfront; apart from cutting the bread, it would be a handy weapon at close quarters. I joined my comrades, and by dawn, there were about three hundred soldiers and most of the officers, including the CO, but there was no sign of Captain Pickering.

We wasted all night in the wood, it was impossible to move during daylight, so we had another day of waiting. I made more enemies than friends trying to share those loaves and cold soup among so many men.

The next evening, the officers decided we would split into two parties and try to make it to the coast. It was a nightmare of a night. Our sense of direction was lacking. The last straw was when my friend Jack North fell and sprained his ankle. With his arm over my shoulder, I managed to support him as he hobbled along, but it was only a matter of time before he became immobile. No way was I going to leave him, so I struggled on; what a relief when the dawn came and we had to find shelter.

We persuaded a farmer to let us use his barn, but we had barely settled down when he rushed in to tell us there was a German tank coming up the drive. He opened a door leading into the field and we all dashed through it. There was no time to take Jack. I just hoped the Germans wouldn't find him in the straw.

It was a sunny day and we soon settled down to sleep in the cornfield. I woke about midday. Everything was quiet at the farm and I wondered if the Germans had gone. I decided to do a little scouting. A brick wall surrounded the farm. I crept up to it and risked peeping over the top. Six tanks lined the yard, and about thirty Germans stretched out asleep on some straw nearby. There was no sign of any guard. I watched for about ten minutes. There wasn't a movement, but then I saw the farmer and managed to attract his attention.

As well as I could by sign language, I asked about Jack. He gesticulated that his ankle was very swollen, and that he was sleeping. When I pointed to the barn and suggested I carry him out, he waved me away, and if I read his signs right he would look after him. I crept back to the cornfield and I told the officer what I'd seen. There was a conference about what we should do. A sergeant voiced his opinion. He was in favour of every man for himself, as we didn't stand a chance together.

'If you are confident you can reach the coast, why don't you earn your stripes by taking some of these young lads with you?' There was a murmur of approval when I suggested that anyone who felt confident should take eight or nine men.

I had eight men with me and after dusk, we set off at five-minute intervals; our party was the eleventh to leave.

It was a beautiful night, and the North Star was easy to pick out as we followed it. When we reached a road, we had a disagreement: some of the party wanted to follow the road because it was easier walking. I explained that we'd spent the previous night following roads and got nowhere.

Climbing the fence I said, 'I'm going due north across country, just please yourselves.' They all followed.

After about three hours of hard slog, we reached a village on the coast. It was deserted; even the cats and dogs had gone. None of the houses were locked, perhaps it was better to leave them open than have the doors broken down. We didn't find any food apart from some carrots, which tasted like a feast. There was no sign of the other parties so we made our way to the beach; that too was deserted.

We investigated a building that stood by the water's edge. It was a coastguard station, and from the top of the building, there was a wonderful view out to sea.

Our navy looked quite close, probably about five miles away. Looking round I found a candle and a metal box with a lid. Lighting the candle in the box, then opening and shutting the lid to make dots and dashes of the Morse code, I tried to send a message to the navy. It was hopeless and I gave up, but the idea still lingered. As daylight broke, I went to the nearest house and fetched two white pillowcases and two curtain poles. Using these to make two flags, I started signalling again and sent a message: *Nine Engineers stranded.* After a while, they returned the message: *Hang on, watch and wait.*

During this time, two or three parties had arrived, and I told a sergeant about the message I'd received and added, 'If they do try to take us off, I don't think it will be before tonight, so I'm going.'

'Where to?' he said.

'I can't wait until tonight; I'm going to Calais or die in the attempt,' I said impulsively.

I set off along a path running parallel with the beach, first running, running a little and then walking. I was making good progress and everything seemed peaceful as I hurried on my way to Calais. Suddenly, a number of shots shattered the tranquillity. Germans were firing at me from the high ground overlooking the beach. I started running, varying my speed to spoil their aim. A thought crossed my mind, 'What lousy shots,' when I felt a stinging pain in my arm just above the wrist. Blood was dripping off my fingers; that probably made me run faster and then the firing stopped.

There were still sounds of firing ahead and as I rounded a bend, I could see a line of men in blue uniforms with red pompoms on their hats. They were French sailors, holding the high ground, and I hoped they would hang on until I passed. My luck ran out as the French came bounding down the hill onto the beach taking me with them. At that moment, a German tank made its way onto the beach, giving us a burst of machine gun fire. I dived for the only bit of cover I could see, a small crevasse in between two rocks. A huge French sailor hit me in mid air as he dived for that same cover. When I last saw him, he was jammed in between the rocks unable to get out.

Capture

We were ordered to line up on the beach with me at the end of the line, and a young officer climbed out of the tank and strode down the line counting in German. When he reached me, he said in perfect English, 'Five hundred frogs and one Englishman, what a bag.'

He insisted I went with him to the tank. It was obvious he was waiting for someone to march us away. He asked which part of England I came from. Instead of saying Derbyshire or Chesterfield, I named the village of Stanfree and added, 'You don't know where that is.'

'Oh! But I do,' he said, and he reeled off the names of every town and village between Derby and Stanfree with a description of the road. He mentioned Markham Colliery and the Coalite Plant at Shuttlewood, adding they wouldn't be there much longer. As he spoke, a fleet of huge trucks arrived, and the French prisoners herded into them.

The German officer put his hand on my arm. 'You stay here, you're alright,' he said.

When I asked how he knew so much about England, he told me he'd been a racing driver at Donington Park, until just before the war.

He turned to me and said, 'Just imagine, very soon you will be in Berlin and I'll be in London.'

'And we'll both be prisoners. That's your only hope of going to London,' I retorted, before he picked me up bodily, and put me on the front mudguard of a lorry that was just moving off.

I found myself clinging to a metal flag post, gripping it for dear life as the lorry lurched and bounced over rough ground. When we reached the road, the ride was smoother, but the overgrown hedges were a new hazard. The first one we encountered nearly dragged me off the mudguard, and seeing my plight, the driver really enjoyed himself. I was on the point of letting go, when we approached a town. It was either Calais or Boulogne, I didn't know which; I'd been too busy hanging on to notice the direction. I soon realised it was Boulogne when the driver pulled up with a jerk, and I was flung into the road. The driver laughed as I picked myself up. Suddenly he stopped and jumped down from his cab and rushed at me. Instinctively I put my hands up to defend myself. It was then he saw the blood from the wound on my arm and he stopped dead. Pointing to my arm, he started jabbering in German. Then I saw what had made him so angry. On one mudguard, a red and white swastika flag fluttered in the breeze and on the other, a blood soaked piece of rag hung limply. By gripping the flagpole so hard, I'd caused the wound on my arm to start bleeding again, and it had spoiled his precious flag.

We were herded into a large factory building. When I saw the tramlines on the floor I realised it was a tram depot. The place was crowded with both English and French soldiers and sailors. I checked all around looking at different faces to see if I could find Jack North. I couldn't see him; perhaps the French farmer had looked after him.

For the first time I had a chance to examine my arm. After I'd washed it under a cold-water tap, I saw it wasn't a bullet, but a piece of rock still embedded in my arm. I wondered how to get it out; then remembered the boning knife stashed down my shirtfront. The Germans had searched me down both sides, but they'd missed the knife in the middle.

It was a painful operation, and I daren't trust anyone else. After I'd managed to dig out the pea-sized rock, and put on a field dressing, it felt much easier.

I mingled with the other men and listened to their conversation; rumour was rife that the Germans were not taking any prisoners. One man was moaning that he'd not had anything to eat all day, which started me thinking what I'd eaten during the past two days: one turnip, a few carrots and a dry crust.

By the time morning arrived, I felt like volunteering for the firing squad, cramped from sitting on the tramlines and tired of standing. The doors of the tram depot swung open and about twenty Germans burst in shouting, *Rouse!*

They held rifles and bayonets in front of them and they forced us back in a tight group at the far end of the tram depot. Some civilians arrived with baskets of sliced bread, a large tin of jam and buckets of coffee.

The Germans released us one by one to collect two slices of bread, a spoonful of jam and a mug of coffee. The German guard was there to see there was no two-timing. While we were eating, a German officer entered with a French and English interpreter. He told us that after breakfast we had to fall into three ranks. We would march twenty kilometres and then get a meal. Anyone breaking ranks would be shot.

There was a lot of speculation when we set off as to our destination. Once we were clear of Boulogne, I looked up and down the column, trying to assess how many prisoners there were. The column stretched as far as the eye could see forward and to the rear. After two hours, we halted for a rest, and as I sat on the grass verge, I noticed the cables for the German field telephones. I couldn't resist hacking through them with my knife. When we fell in again ready to move off, there was a roar of laughter all around me. I'd taken my boots and socks off and hung them round my neck. I knew the consequences of marching long distances in army boots in hot weather. One witty fellow shouted, 'Are you saving them for church parade?' Before we finished that march, the majority of them had followed suit, but too late, they were all limping.

We had walked more than twenty kilometres, but there was no sign of a meal. The guards told us in sign language, another five and then another. I believe we marched thirty-five kilometres before turning off the road into a field. In one corner was a field kitchen with the fires blazing. I heard the announcement, 'Have your mess tins ready. No mess tin, no soup.'

I didn't have a mess tin, but this wasn't the time to be fussy. I remembered seeing a French soldier lying in the hedgerow as I turned in the gateway to the field. He was dead and his steel helmet was by his side. I picked it up and tore the lining out. I never thought I'd eat soup out of a dead man's hat.

The English and French formed into two separate columns. The French were to go first, and they started filing past the field kitchen collecting a mess tin of soup and a slice of bread. It seemed the French column was endless – until the English lads realised the French were going round for second helpings. They rushed forward and bowled the French out of the way. Unfortunately, they bowled what was left of the soup over as well. Hungry and weary, we huddled together to try to keep warm. The day had been so hot, but the night was bitterly cold.

Next morning we were on the march again without food or drink. While we were resting at the first halt that day, a lorry drove down a side road and stopped. Another batch of English soldiers jumped out. A roar of laughter went up when they saw one of them dressed in just vest and pants. Someone shouted, 'Did they catch you in bed?'

When we fell in ready to march off, I stood by the side of this fellow.

'Some of you would laugh if your mother's arse was on fire,' he said. Then he turned to me and inquired, 'I suppose you've come to find out how I managed to be dressed like this?'

'No, I'm not that curious. I just wanted to let you have my overcoat,' I said, passing it to him.

'What makes you take pity on me, it's pretty obvious I've no cigarettes?' he queried.

'I don't know yet. I'll tell you when I've made my mind up.'

We carried on talking until I finally asked him where he thought we were going. He looked around and said, 'I don't know about this lot, but the first opportunity, I'm getting the hell out of here.'

'Now, I've made my mind up why I gave you my overcoat. When you are in a situation like this, it's nice to have someone you can depend on. You looked that type and from your conversation, I think you are.' That was the beginning of my friendship with Alex Jenkins; a friendship tested many times.

Alex came from Liverpool, married, with one son that he'd not seen. He was a driver in the Royal Army Service Corps, until the Germans had caught up with him at St. Valery. Removing his clothes, he'd swum out to a boat that was at anchor. Just when he reached the boat heading out to sea, the Germans started shelling. One shell fell so close to the boat that it overturned. Hours later, still clinging to the boat, he was washed ashore about twenty miles further down the coast.

We spent the night at a sports ground, where they gave us two small ladles of soup, which just covered the bottom of my steel helmet and a loaf of bread to share between thirty of us. It was a hot, sultry night, but it looked as though there would be a storm, so all the

English lads decided to shelter in a pavilion. It was terribly hot and uncomfortable, but we would be dry if the storm arrived. The French opted to sleep outside on the grass, but halfway through the night, when the rain teemed down, they tried to fight their way into the pavilion. The German guards eventually broke up the fighting by firing warning shots into the air. Fortunately, no one was hurt, but both sides looked worse for wear next morning.

The march was beginning to take its toll. Many men collapsed, and if they didn't get up after a beating, they were thrown on a wagon. My hunger disappeared, now superseded by thirst. The following days became a nightmare because when civilians put buckets of water on the side of the road, in the rush they were overturned.

Just a few incidents stuck in my mind: for instance, the day when one of our fellows was shot through the stomach when he came out of a garden, with his arms full of rhubarb. The guard who shot him said he was trying to escape. That would have made sense had he been going, but he was coming back. He was the lad I went into Boulogne with before the Germans arrived. I remembered the things he was going to do when he returned home. I thought of the French woman's offer to take us in her car to the South of France; how I wished that we'd gone. Another unforgettable incident was the day we passed a village pond; a coating of moss, leaves and feathers covered it. Despite warning shots from the guards, we made a dive for that pond. It looked filthy, but it tasted like wine.

The last day of the march was the most gruelling. It started with the usual tactics. Only so many miles, and then just a few more until eventually we arrived in Trier on the Belgium Luxemburg frontier. A very steep hill led us up to a fort, where we were to spend the night. As we passed through the gate, I saw some loaves of bread piled in a basket. I reached out and grabbed one as I passed. It was a small loaf, and I cut it in five slices and passed four to those nearest me. A man behind me started grumbling because I hadn't given him a slice, and one of the guards, a big Prussian fellow heard. He thrust at me with his bayonet and I sidestepped him, but he then swung his rifle round and caught me on the arm with the butt. The searing pain made me feel sick. I felt sure my arm was broken. If there was any consolation, it was my left arm and not my right.

After a sleepless night, we were marched to a railway siding and loaded into cattle trucks, bound for an unknown destination. All day and well into the night we travelled, and by the sunlight shining through the cracks during the day, we'd been going east. This seemed to please Alex. 'The further they go in that direction the better,' he said. I wasn't so sure.

Eventually, we arrived at our destination, a place called Szubin, somewhere in Poland. When I saw the camp, it sent a chill through my veins. There was a double fence of barbed wire with a soldier sitting behind a machine gun in a crow's nest at each corner. From time to time, he swivelled the gun just to let us know he was awake.

As it was breaking daylight, we were herded sixty to each large hut. We hadn't time to settle down before the door opened and a German guard entered, accompanied by a sergeant out of the 'King's Rules and Regulations'.

Everyone had passed remarks about him licking Gerry's boots all the way on the march. He never seemed to queue for his drop of soup. Obviously he was getting his on the side. The German guard had four loaves of bread under his arm, and these he flung into the centre of the floor. Having had nothing to eat since we left Trier, the men were fighting each other for the crumbs. I stood back and saw the sergeant, with a look of contempt on his face, shouting, 'You're like a lot of pigs!' I reckon you're the biggest pig of all, because your belly is full and theirs is empty, I thought.

Later that day, we were numbered, photographed and thumb printed. I became *Kriegsgefangener* No. 2426, and given a letter card to write to my wife. What could I say? I felt degraded, broken in body, disillusioned by some of my fellow men, but thank God, my spirit was intact.

It was a relief to get some treatment for my arm. I was marched to a small hospital where an American doctor said my arm wasn't broken, but the ligaments were damaged. While he was examining my arm, he whispered some news. France was about finished and unless the Americans joined in, the war was almost over.

We had our first real meal for about a fortnight. Stew with cabbage and potatoes boiled in their jackets, cooked by Polish POWs. Before the meal had finished I overheard some of the men grumbling that they could cook it better. Peeling the potatoes would be an improvement.

'Want a bet?' I asked Alex, 'if they get their hands in, we won't get half this amount in future.'

My forecast came true. Some of our lads approached the Germans and got themselves installed as cooks. I must admit, the stew was leaner and the potatoes peeled, but the quantity had dropped.

I turned to Alex and said, 'What with barbed wire, machine gun posts, search lights and now the Devil's kitchen, when are we getting out of here?'

With a grin on his face, he said, 'Tomorrow. I've just put our names down for a working party.'

'Where is that going to take us, Russia?'

'No, Sommerlager. Wherever that is.'

Next morning after a breakfast of a small dry loaf between five, washed down with black coffee, we packed into a huge lorry bound for Sommerlager. After a two-hour journey, we left the main road and turned along what looked like a cart track. After travelling about seven miles without seeing a house or a person, we passed a cavalry camp. Half a mile further on the lorry rumbled to a halt; this was Sommerlager.

It was a hundred yards square, fenced in with barbed wire with two army huts in the centre. Alex and I agreed it didn't look very promising. It was more remote than Salisbury Plain, but at least there were no machine gun posts or searchlights.

We were set to work digging ditches for drainage on either side of the road. We lined up to march to work on the second morning, and had a very unpleasant surprise when told to take our boots off and place them in front of us. We were marched to a lorry that had just arrived at the gate, and handed two square pieces of cloth and a pair of wooden clogs. You could say we hobbled to work, while the lorry collected our boots and drove off. It was surprising how soon everyone got used to those clogs and it wasn't long before we were having clog races.

Alex and I became friends with a chap called Jim Smart, who came from North London. He often talked of a boxing club to which he belonged and how he missed it. We never took him seriously until one day when an Irish lad called John Morrison, nicknamed Bomber, was having an argument with a big fellow who had taken his rations. This fellow was a noted bully and he asked Bomber what he was going to do about it. Jim Smart went up to him and asked, 'Why don't you pick on someone your own size?' That caused a laugh because the bully was head and shoulders taller than Jim was. The laughing must have annoyed him because he took a swipe, and everyone gasped as Jim ducked and then hit the big fellow three or four times then danced away. It was like watching a bullfight, with the big fellow rushing in and flailing the air, and Jim bobbing up and hitting him two or three times before dancing away again. It was a marvellous exhibition of boxing. After that fight, the bully stopped his bullying. That was how Bomber came to join us, and the four of us became inseparable.

Sommerlager did little to further our plans for escape, apart from Alex learning to speak German. A spate of disease, due to an open trench that served as a toilet, had the camp closed down and back we went to Szubin.

By this time, the Szubin camp was really organised. The sergeant major and his band of followers had a nice little number with Red Cross parcels and clothing from England; we felt like intruders into their domain.

It was inevitable I was going to run into trouble the first mealtime. I joined the queue for my stew with my old helmet. Long before I reached the head of the queue, I could see the procedure. If you were one of the boys, down went the ladle and you got meat and vegetables, otherwise the ladle skimmed the top, and you got water. The man in front of me was one of the boys, and down went the ladle. The sergeant major looked at me, and skimmed the top. It looked like dirty dishwater. I didn't find out what it tasted like, I just teemed it back in the dixie. He called to one of the guards. I was marched off and for the rest of the day and night, I was locked in a windowless hut. Next morning I was before the commandant, and then sent for two days in X Company. I never saw anyone else in X Company; only the guard who brought me dry bread and water. I spent two days in that wooden hut in darkness, with no bedding.

Alex met me when I came out. He'd put our names on the working party list, to build a new camp near

Poznan. He'd managed to find out quite a lot of information from one of the guards. We were going to turn a village school into a POW camp, which was to be known as Stalag XXIB.

We travelled from Szubin to Poznan on an ordinary passenger train, with a guard in each compartment: fifty POWs and six guards. The carriages were similar to those in England. Facing me on the wall were pictures of places of interest in Poznan and a map. I memorised the map, noting apprehensively that the river ran through the city, and the position of the railway lines. A river meant bridges and bridges meant guards. We were taken by lorry from Poznan to the village about ten kilometres away.

The school consisted of four classrooms: two downstairs and two up, with a central stairway. The first task was to erect barbed wire fences round the school playground. Alex and I were the first to volunteer for that job. Our idea to leave a wire unfastened was soon spotted by the guard. There was no chance of losing the wire cutters; the guard wouldn't let them out of his sight. We had almost finished fixing the wire fence. There was one section behind the toilets to complete, when I had an idea.

Alex was on good terms with the guard, who was eager to learn English. Therefore, I told him to suggest to the guard that we could put perpendicular wires as well as horizontal behind the toilets.

'Tell him it would make it more difficult for the Poles to throw parcels of food through', I suggested to Alex. The guard fell for it; he thought it was a good idea. I thought so too. When we'd finished, those upright strands had made a good ladder.

Our way out was settled, now we had to consider the rest of our plans. The sketch I'd drawn showed that the railway branched in five different directions from Poznan, so if we were going to jump a train, and that seemed our only hope, it would be better to jump one east of Poznan.

As soon as the camp was completed, another batch of POWs arrived to fill all the rooms, and we were set to work making a new road. Lorries brought loads of gravestones, mostly from Polish Jewish graves, and we had to break them up to surface the road.

Escape

O ur plans began to take shape. We had the means
  to get out of the camp, and we had to get on a
train east of Poznan, with the hope of getting to Russia.
The obvious day to escape was a Saturday, after the roll
call at approximately six o'clock in the evening. There
wasn't another roll call until the following Monday
morning.

When Alex and I began to save a portion of our
bread ration each day this caused Bomber and Jim to
inform us they too were in on the mission.

Jim Smart had been having problems with ulcers on
his legs for quite a long time, and without treatment,
they were getting worse. One morning he couldn't
stand on his legs, and when called out for work, he just
stayed on his bed. The sergeant major reported one
man was lame and couldn't walk. The commander
dashed into the room, followed by the guards, and we
could hear the swish of his riding crop as he gave poor
Jim a beating. When this was to no avail, they followed
with the usual pattern of threatening to shoot him. I
heard the rattle of their rifle bolts. Suddenly I realised
one man could be shot accidentally, but not four.

'Aren't we all in this together?'

'Bet your life we are!' said Bomber as we went back
into the room and sat beside Jim. The guard
commander looked like an over privileged turkey cock,

as he ranted at us in German. I said to Alex, 'When he stops for breath, tell him we're not going to work until Jim gets some treatment for his leg.'

Eventually Alex managed to get a word in, and the German looked taken aback. Then he gave an order, which the guards translated into deeds, and we were bundled outside and into a coal store. The door slammed, and we were left to grope in the darkness to find out what sort of place we had landed.

The store was about eight foot by six, with a damp brick floor; nothing to lie or sit on. There was a piece of wood nailed to the wall and we managed to pull this off, to make a rough seat. It wasn't comfortable, but it was better than the floor. The hours seemed like days, it was impossible to monitor the time. We discussed everything, including our plans to escape, which now seemed hopeless.

The guard brought us dry bread and a jug of water. Alex asked him the time, but received no answer. As the night wore on, we had to keep moving about to keep our circulation going. Sleep was out of the question. The door remained locked until the following morning when we were marched into the commandant's office.

A German officer, brought in to deal with us, sat at a table. The officer read out the charge in perfect English, and went on to explain that mutiny applied to POWs the same as soldiers. 'Which of you is the ringleader?' he asked.

'We don't need a ringleader, we're all in this together, and you can do what you will, we're not going to work until Jim gets some treatment for his legs,' I answered.

He stood up and walked round the table, 'Let me have a look at your leg,' he said to Jim.

When he saw the ulcers, he turned to the commandant. I thought he was going to strike him as he raved in German. The commandant clicked his heels and dashed out; and the officer turned to Jim and told him a car was coming to take him to hospital.

Then he said to us, 'There are good and bad in every nation. You can go now and tomorrow you will go to work.' As we left he added, 'I think you are brave men.'

We received a double ration of soup for dinner, and later in the afternoon, Jim came back from hospital with a large parcel of dressings for his legs.

Later that week, a load of boots arrived from the Red Cross and they replaced our wooden clogs. As Alex tried his new boots, he asked, 'What are we waiting for? I think it's time for us to get out.'

So that one of us could pass for a civilian, Alex persuaded one of the sailors to change overcoats and we covered the buttons with cloth. We unpicked a strip off a woollen patchwork quilt for a scarf and when the commandant's trousers were hanging on the washing line to dry, we stole them.

Our plans were finalised after watching the German movements at the last roll call before locking the doors at night. The commandant and a guard came into the two ground floor rooms and everyone had to stand by their beds, then they would go to the upstairs rooms. When they came back downstairs, everyone had to be in bed. After looking around the room, they would switch the lights out and lock the outer doors.

Our plan was, after the Germans went upstairs we would go outside and hide in the corner near the toilets, leaving our beds so that it would look like we were still sleeping in them. When the commandant and guard had left, we would go over the wire one by one, in between the guards' patrol of the camp.

The day of escape was arranged for Saturday 6th December, and as the day drew near we found it difficult to keep it secret, but we realised it would be dangerous to let anyone know until the last minute.

On the day before the planned escape, Jim Smart surprised us by announcing that he wasn't going with us. His legs had not healed, and he felt he would be an encumbrance. He insisted he was going outside with us to keep watch. Then after we'd left, he'd tell the guard that he'd slipped out to the toilet, and been locked out. We pointed out that it wasn't necessary, but he was adamant. We realised he wanted to have a hand in our getaway, so we let him have his way.

I don't think any of us had much sleep that night, we were too keyed up. By Saturday afternoon, the other men knew we were definitely going to try to escape. This was all because I had a shave. This isn't unusual unless you haven't had one for more than seven months.

When I was taken prisoner, I had a safety razor and one blade, and I vowed I'd use it the day I escaped. It was a painful process, and I made another vow, I'd never grow another beard.

While Alex was trying on his outfit of grey trousers and blue overcoat, the sergeant came to us. He looked so worried and lost for words.

Suddenly, he blurted out, 'I don't think you realise what you're doing.' For a moment I thought he was concerned about us, until he said, 'You don't care what happens to us. They are bound to take it out on us when they find you've gone.'

I reminded him it was a soldier's duty to try to escape, and reassured him the Germans would probably close the canteen for a week and there was very little to buy anyway, only rubbish.

Later that afternoon, I found my knife was missing. Everyone borrowed it and returned it, but not today. I asked everyone, but to no avail. It would have been a handy weapon as a last resort, but evidently, someone had a better use for it.

We were hoping for a dull night with a wind to deaden the sounds. That is how the weather was until about five o'clock and then it started to snow, rain and blow. On a night like that, roll call was a mere formality, just a quick walk up and down the room to check everyone was present. As soon as the guards had gone upstairs, we made our beds to look like they were occupied, and then we slipped outside. The roll call over, the guards locked the door and went to their quarters. Jim gave us the tip; the guard was going away from us on his patrol of the camp.

Bomber started to climb the wire. He made hard work of it, instead of feeling his way from wire to wire; he seemed to be dancing on them. The plan was to go over in turn, but Alex decided to go while Bomber was still struggling.

Time seemed endless as I waited for them to clear the wire, and I resigned myself to waiting for the guard to come round again. Jim gave me the tip to go, so obviously the guard was taking his time or sheltering from the weather. I was halfway up when Jim said, 'Make haste, he's coming!' Instead of feeling my way to avoid the spikes of the barbed wire, I had to hurry, regardless of tearing my hands to shreds. As I got clear of the wire, I heard Jim calling to the guard to tell him he'd been locked out.

We had agreed to rendezvous at a haystack about four hundred yards away and as each one approached we were to give a bird whistle which would be answered. I thought the other two would be at the haystack before me, so when I gave the whistle, I wasn't surprised when it was promptly answered. As I rounded the corner of the haystack, and came face to face with a figure in the darkness, instinct told me it wasn't Alex or Bomber. I grabbed the figure by the throat and pushed his head in the straw. Perhaps it was for the best that I'd lost my knife, otherwise he might have been dead when Alex and Bomber arrived. As I released my hold on him, he gasped, *'Polak'*. We knew about five words of Polish and that was one of them.

Fortunately, he could speak German and Alex explained we'd escaped from the camp and told him to forget that he'd seen us.

We set off across country knowing that sooner or later we would get to the railway line. The weather, which had favoured our getaway, now made life uncomfortable. The southeast wind blowing in our faces cut us like a knife.

We seemed to have been walking for hours when we reached the railway; we turned to the east to follow it. After walking along the line for two or three kilometres, we heard a train approaching from behind, and crouched down while it passed. It was slowing down, but not enough for us to be able to jump on. Another three hundred yards and we would have made it, for it slowed to walking pace as it rumbled over the bridge. There was no need to go any nearer; the sentry was plainly visible in the light of the engine. We had to try to find some shelter and wait for another train.

A platelayer's hut about twenty yards back from the line seemed an ideal spot. Sleep was impossible, but taking it in turns, two rested while the other kept watch for a train.

As they settled down Alex turned to Bomber and said, 'Get the smokes out.'

Bomber jumped to his feet. In his anger, the Irish brogue was plain to hear, 'Mother of God! Are you telling me you haven't brought them?' What a body blow. Those two would rather have a cigarette than a slice of bread.

It was a fruitless watch and dawn broke. We waited for darkness again before we could risk trying to board a train. After breakfast of what would have been dry bread, had it not been for the rain, we settled down to wait.

It was fortunate for us it was Sunday and there were no workers about, but we had a shock when we heard footsteps outside and a man opened the door. He was terrified when he saw us, and would have bolted had I not grabbed him. Under Alex's questioning, he said he was Polish and a foreman in charge of a gang of platelayers, and on Sunday, he came to check the tools. Once again, we had to take a chance and let him go. He warned us to be out by dawn as the men started work early. After shaking hands with him and a cigarette for Alex and Bomber, he hurried away.

During the afternoon, Alex announced he was going to have a scout round. Perhaps it was to test his attire in public, but I wished it had been for a more useful mission than looking for cigarettes. He returned safely, his mission successful. Somehow, he'd acquired two packets.

As soon as it was dark we positioned ourselves by the railway line, and only just in time, because before we had settled down to wait, we heard the rumbling of a train. Alex gave Bomber a few hints on how to get on the train, but it didn't help, for when I scrambled into the first wagon and looked round for Bomber he was hanging on the side of a wagon, and couldn't pull himself up. Jumping off, I gave him a lift up, and only just managed to get on myself in the wagon next to the guard van. Fortunately, the guard was looking out on the other side. After we'd crossed the river, I started working my way back from wagon to wagon. It was a slow moving train, and I'd a feeling we were not on the main Warsaw line. Alex, who had come to join me, was in the same mind.

'Let's be thankful we're over the river and each mile is further away from that camp.' At that moment, the train shuddered to a halt.

We could see a railway siding when we peeped over the top of the wagon. After a few minutes, we heard the engine moving away without us. The sidings were deserted. We had no idea where we were, so we climbed out of the wagons and followed the railway line.

It was a bitterly cold night. Fortunately, our clothes had dried out, but Bomber wasn't very happy. We hadn't gone far when he exclaimed, 'I hope you don't think I'm walking to Russia.'

Alex, who was leading, stopped dead and turned to Bomber, 'If I'm not mistaken there is a little box ahead with a sentry, so now's your chance to give yourself up.'

There was an awkward silence as we moved away from the railway line, but Bomber followed us. Following a track, we came to a river and the bridge over it was plainly visible; so too was the red glow of the sentry's cigarette.

The railway had been going southeast, but now following the river, we were going north or northeast;

but we had no choice. Alex with his long stride had Bomber struggling to keep up with him, so I took the lead.

Twice we saw a wide ditch running away from the river, obviously to take the floodwater. Everywhere, the soil was like silver sand and with the moon shining on it, and it gave the impression of water. We carefully felt our way in case it was water and not solid ground. I stepped and suddenly went up to the shoulders in icy water. Alex and Bomber dragged me out of the ditch; there was no alternative but to carry on, but I knew that very shortly I'd have to shelter.

We arrived at a small village and choosing the poorest looking house, we knocked on the door. The sound of voices inside told us they were not German, and after a few minutes the door opened and a very old man stood holding a lantern. As the light fell on Alex, the man drew back, and then his lantern shone on Bomber and me. '*Americanski*' he shouted, and flung the door wide open and beckoned us in. Not wishing to create a wrong impression we tried our best to tell him we were English, but he couldn't understand either English or German. He kept muttering, '*Americanski, dobsher,*' and we knew that meant 'Americans, good.' Therefore, we left it at that.

With straw and wood, he soon had a fire burning in the stove at the far end of the room. While he put a saucepan of milk on the stove and chunks of pork in the frying pan, I looked round the room for his wife. Huddled in a corner, looking terrified was a little boy about eight years old. He refused to come out until the old man reassured him. While we were eating the best meal we'd had for more than six months, I took stock of the house.

It was one long room, the door in one end and the stove at the other. A small window on either side, with sacks hung over them to shield the light. Two small beds either side of the stove, a table and two wooden stools completed the furniture. The rattle of a chain at the other end of the room caused us all to jump to our feet. The old man motioned us to sit down; we couldn't understand a word he was saying. He raised the lantern from the table, and the ray of light shone on a horse and two goats at the other end of the room.

My thoughts went back to the miner's home where I stayed in Durham. That was poor, but what could I call this? Yet the hospitality was the same. It seemed the world over, the poor were the most generous.

When we'd finished eating, the old man pointed to the beds but we pointed to the straw and then he fetched a bale and put it in the corner. It was then he noticed my wet clothes, and gave me a long nightshirt to wear while he took my clothes and put them to dry.

The sound of voices woke us. There was a stranger in the room talking to our benefactor. He came over to us and spoke in German. Alex answered him and they had quite a conversation before he turned to us and apologised in perfect in English, explaining that he wanted to be sure we were genuine, because the Germans could play some cunning tricks.

He'd brought a map of Poland and he pointed out where we were, what dangers to look out for and the best route to follow. It appeared the river we'd crossed at Poznan was the same river we were following now: the River Warte, and we had to cross it again. He told us where we would find someone with a boat to take us across the river. Then he wrote out a note in Polish to give to any Pole when we needed help. It read: *To good Polish citizens, these men are our English friends. Give them what help you can for the sake of our country.*

He spent the rest of the day until dusk talking to us of the war, our country and our homes. I asked him how an old man and a young boy came to be living together in such conditions. He explained: The old man, with his daughter and son-in-law had a good farm and a nice house before the war, but the Germans had taken the house and the best land, and given it to a fellow German. His daughter and son-in-law had been taken for forced labour in Germany, leaving the young boy with the old man.

When it was time to leave, the old man gave us a sack of freshly baked bread for the journey. We gave our thanks and said goodbye. Tears ran down his cheeks as his parting words were translated: *Tell your people, the Germans have our land and money, but they will never have our spirit.*

The man led us through the village and along a path by the river. He pointed out the direction to take and offered us his hand, saying, 'I've helped you all I can; now I wish you good luck.'

How much better we felt now, after a good feed and rest. Soon Alex was striding out, and I was commuting from one to the other, slowing one down and hastening the other. It was while we were waiting for Bomber to catch up we saw two policemen walking towards us. We quickly turned off the road and hid in some bushes. A small stream was running through the bushes and we crouched down beside it. Bomber had joined us by this time, and when he took hold of the sack of bread I was carrying, I thought he was being helpful. When we were sure the Germans had gone, we turned back on to the road. Alex let out such a roar. Bomber was sitting comfortably on the sack of bread that was in the stream. They'd not been on been on very good terms since getting over the wire and I had to remind them we were trying to reach Russia not conducting a feud.

We walked on for as long as we dare but we had to have shelter before daylight. Even the well-worded note didn't work miracles. At the first house we tried, a woman answered the door and Alex handed her the note. She read it and looked undecided, then she handed it back and quickly slammed the door. As the silver streaks of day were beginning to show, we decided that the next farm we found we would just creep into the barn.

There was a farm on the outskirts of a village. There was no sign of anyone, so we assumed the owners must be in bed. As we settled in the barn, I remarked to Alex that there was something queer about the place. He always said, 'Poland is the land of barking dogs,' but no dog had barked.

Quietly, I went to the farmhouse and tried the door. It was open and I went inside: not a soul in sight. There was no food, clothes or bedding. Back in the barn, I relayed this to Alex and Bomber and they were all for moving in to the farm.

'No, let's stay here, it will be safer.' I was remembering how the old man had lost his farm and family, and I'd a feeling the same thing was happening here.

We climbed onto a pile of hay and made ourselves comfortable. The sound of horses approaching and then voices interrupted our sleep. Alex peeped through a hole in the wood of the barn. A cart brimming with household goods had stopped at the door and three men and two women were chattering excitedly in German.

Alex turned to me and said, 'You are right; the swine have won a farm.'

We fell asleep again until someone pulled the hay underneath where we slept. Wide-awake now and ready to spring, we waited hoping they would take some hay and go away. The dust from the hay must have got under Bomber's nose for he was about to sneeze when we grabbed him. With my hand over his mouth, and Alex holding his nose, he turned blue in the face. As the man left the barn, we let him go.

'That was a bit close,' whispered Alex.

'You squeezed the living daylights out of me,' gasped Bomber.

The rest of the day passed without further incidents, sleeping and eating what would have been dry bread, but for Bomber dunking it in the stream.

Once more, we set off on our journey. We traced the route on our map, but the names of the villages had been changed to German. The village was Pydzdry. The weather was changing; a few snowflakes blew in the wind and made us turn our collars up.

We didn't see the policeman until it was too late. Fortunately, we were on the opposite side of the road, and I still wonder if the Lord prompted us, as we raised our arms in the Nazi salute and shouted, *'Heil Hitler.'* The policeman returned the salute and walked on; that was the closest shave so far.

The weather had become atrocious. We had to link arms for two reasons, the blizzard meant we could lose each other and there was a large ditch either side of the road. We realised we would have to find shelter, but where? With visibility so poor we wouldn't see a house if we passed one.

Eventually we saw a light and made towards it, but it vanished. Groping our way forward we heard a whirring sound above the storm. A few minutes later, a gust of wind almost knocked us off our feet. I felt rather sick as I realised we'd almost walked into the sails of a windmill. Turning away, we stumbled into a fence, and feeling our way along the fence we came to a gate. It was then we saw a chink of light and hurried forward in case it disappeared.

The light was shining through a small window and we hammered on the window frame until a door opened and a man, presumably the miller, appeared holding a lantern. As the light fell on us, he yelled with delight, '*Americanski*' and ushered us into the house. It was then we noticed the miller's face. He had a handkerchief wrapped round his face; I thought to keep out the cold, but now I could see he had no nose. He seemed embarrassed, so we didn't ask questions, but we'd a feeling it wasn't the work of a surgeon.

After giving us a meal, he took us to the bedroom where two spotlessly clean beds looked so inviting. It was almost a year since I'd slept in a proper bed. Resisting the temptation, we used sign language to tell him we would rather sleep in the barn.

He took us to the barn and pointed to a ladder, which we climbed. We fell exhausted onto a stack of straw and, in spite of the sound of the windmill sails, we slept.

The Rewers Family

We woke to the sound of a voice shouting, 'Hello! Come down here, I want to talk to you.'

Peeping down I saw the miller had a man with him. The fur-lined coat gave the appearance of a Polish farmer, but his voice had an American accent.

'Come up here if you want to talk to us,' I said, and he made his way up the ladder.

He didn't ask us who we were, or where we came from. For about ten minutes, he asked us general knowledge questions on England and America. Evidently satisfied, he held out his hand and introduced himself as Piotr Rewers, a Polish farmer. He apologised for all the questions, but explained that it was unwise to trust anyone on sight. The miller had braved the storm while we were sleeping to inform Piotr that he had three American soldiers at his house.

Piotr explained that he'd spent a number of years in America before the war. He was a very interesting man, a peasant farmer, who could quote Shakespeare from memory in a perfect American accent. He'd travelled to America to make his fortune working in the slaughter yards in Chicago, but later spent all his savings trying to become a doctor. Unfortunately, his savings ran out before he could qualify, but his medical knowledge proved invaluable in the Polish village of Dziedzice. The death of his mother caused him to return to

Poland, and that was the death of his ambitions. He'd built his own house on western lines, but had to live on the ground floor as the outbreak of war stopped the plastering of the upstairs rooms. His faith in Britain and America was unshakeable; the outcome of the war was definite. His only worry was how long it would take.

He asked us what we'd done and what our plans were. As we explained what we were trying to do, the way he shook his head told us what he thought of our plans.

When we'd finished he said, 'Gentlemen! You don't have a cat in hell's chance.' He asked if we would spend a few days with him, until he could see what he could do to help us. 'Think it over and I'll come back after dark to lead you on your way, or take you to stay with me. So long,' he drawled as he went down the ladder.

The miller's wife brought soup and bread, and once more, we settled down to sleep. It was dark when the miller called us to the house for another meal. Piotr hadn't arrived as promised. The wind had dropped and a few snowflakes were falling. The miller had managed to fasten the sails of the mill. After the meal, we decided to move on. We shook hands with the miller and his wife, and thanked them for their kindness.

There was no sign of Piotr Rewers as we made our way up the road, perhaps he'd had second thoughts about helping us, and who could blame him.

A voice sounded from the direction of some trees, 'So you thought I was a quitter?' inquired Piotr as he stepped out from behind a tree. 'Follow me in single file, and keep in my footsteps or you may fall in a ditch,' he said as he turned off the road.

We followed in silence, somehow I felt I could follow him through a minefield, he seemed to give such confidence. After a while, we arrived at a building surrounded by a high wooden fence. 'This is my brother's farm,' said Piotr. To me it looked more like a fortress than a farm. The gate swung open as we reached it, a man waved us towards the house, and he fastened the gate behind us. The house was in complete darkness, we were all inside and the door shut before the lamp was lit.

Piotr introduced us to the family. There was Piotr's brother Wojciech Rewers and his wife Maria, also two of their children, Jolanta and Slawek. During the introductions, for some unknown reason, Slawek called me Stefan and the name subsequently stuck.

Mrs Rewers (Maria) gave us a sample of her cooking and said via Piotr that this was a very special occasion. We talked late into the night and Piotr outlined his proposals. They would look after us until spring and obtain false identity papers and civilian clothes.

Our bed that night was in the barn, Wojciech was full of apologies for not giving us a bed in the house. The next night when Piotr visited, our decision was a formality; our prospects at that time looked very bleak. He told us, 'Two can stay at my farm, but the other one stays here with Wojciech.'

We all wanted to go with Piotr, which was understandable. The one who stayed would be isolated with not a word of English, the only conversation in sign language. We cut cards to see who stayed with Wojciech. I was the odd man out, so I stayed.

Alex and Bomber left with Piotr, and I went to my bed in the barn, cold and desolate. Wojciech was surprised next morning, when he opening the barn door, to find me walking around. I'm sure if I hadn't kept walking, I'd have frozen to death.

After breakfast he showed me round the farm buildings: one long brick building, two storeys high, comprising the living quarters at one end, two bedrooms, dining room and kitchen next to the stable and cowshed combined. The pigs occupied the rest of the ground floor. The upper floor was one long room used for the storage of grain, hay and a host of other things. The building made one boundary of the farmyard and the barn made another. In between the two was a high gate into the fields; the other two sides were enclosed with a high fence, and another gate opened on to a cart track leading to the road and the village of Dziedzice a mile away.

Wojciech went to great lengths to impress upon me, in sign language, the four escape routes from any part of the main building. There was a trapdoor from the house into the loft, one above the horses' manger, another in the cowshed and a fourth from the pigsty. To all intents and purposes, they were for feeding the animals, but they would prove invaluable for getting out in a hurry. Our tour ended at the dog kennel, and it was there we hit a language barrier. Wojciech tried to explain something about the dog or the kennel or both. On the side of the barn was a brick kennel and Wojciech pointed to the kennel opening, for me to go inside. At the back of the kennel was a hole leading into the barn. I went through this and there was a proper hide-out. Wooden stakes had been leant against the wall to hold the bales of straw back, to make a tunnel. Here and there, a hole in the mortar between the bricks let in a faint chink of light. I began to wonder what sort of man I was staying with; what with trapdoors and hide-outs, perhaps Piotr would put me wise.

Wojciech was a worker and he believed everyone should be the same, and I was no exception. The rest of the week, I was busy from morning until night. Perhaps it was for the best that I was tired out because my change in sleeping quarters after that first night was a surprise.

Instead of cleaning the cowshed out daily, fresh straw was strewn on top of the old: this gave the cow added warmth. It was a shock when my host took me to the cowshed and, after digging a hole and filling it with clean straw, told me in sign language that this was my bed. Beggars can't be choosers and I'd freeze to death in the barn, so I settled down to a sleepless night. What kept me awake were the two chained-up horses and six cows, because every time one moved, the chain rattled; but by the end of the week, I'd have slept if the Devil was chained up next to me.

Sunday was a day of rest, apart from feeding the animals. After breakfast, we heard their dog Mroz bark twice and then disappear into his kennel.

'Piotr,' said Wojciech, and he went to the gate to make sure, while hustling me to hide in the loft, just in case. After half an hour, Piotr called me down and said, 'I've been listening to your countrymen in London on the radio. The news isn't very encouraging.'

Before he left, he told me that Alex and Bomber would visit me after dark, so I spent the day waiting for the sun to set.

What a relief it was to see them again, even to hear their grumbles. They were living in the village and so it wasn't safe for them out of doors during daylight, therefore they were spending their time in the upper rooms of Piotr's house, the part that wasn't finished. It was obvious they were tired of each other's company and bored with nothing to do. They were amazed at the work I was doing and the progress I was making with sign language. It was soon time for them to go, and as I bade them goodnight I realised it was my last word of English for a week.

The following morning Wojciech taught me a new trade. He fetched some thread his wife had spun and a ball of beeswax, and then he showed me how to wax thread. While I was doing that, he fetched a pile of broken harnesses, and I spent three whole days stitching until my fingers ached.

During the weeks before Christmas, I learnt how to milk the cow, make Polish vodka and kill a pig without it squealing. It was much harder learning to speak Polish. I pointed to an object and Wojciech told me the Polish name. The two children, Slawek and Jolanta, were also very helpful. I'd never have progressed beyond farmyard Polish if Piotr hadn't found an old English-Polish dictionary and a Polish history book, which I read repeatedly.

The Rewers family tried to make a happy Christmas for us, but it was difficult. How can you celebrate Christmas when you are counting the days until spring?

The first time a German policeman visited the farm since my arrival was two days after Christmas. Mroz left us in no doubt about the visitor and he let me pass through his kennel to the hide-out beyond without any trouble. It wasn't an official visit, just a bit of scrounging. The German wanted some meat, but all they dare give him was a fowl. Wojciech explained that pigs, sheep and cattle had to be registered and it was a crime to kill them without permission. Young pigs or calves had to be sold or registered as soon as they were old enough, but the Poles would often keep some back and not register them and these were switched between families and friends. Keeping the spare pigs out of sight was a problem. When the police visited and checked the stock, Jolanta and Slawek drove the spare ones out of the back gate into the fields and kept them out of sight. Wojciech's farm seemed to be a hive of illegal industry: killing pigs, making butter, distilling vodka and listening to the radio. All of these activities carried a heavy penalty but it was an accepted way of life and they all seemed to depend on the dog, Mroz. Whenever carrying out anything illegal, he had a special chain with a weak link, so with a sudden snatch he would be loose.

Things started to go wrong about the middle of January. The district overseer arrived accompanied by two policemen and confiscated one of Wojciech's horses. They said he was half an acre of land short to warrant two horses. The following week the one remaining horse took ill. It strained itself pulling a huge cogwheel that drove the machine to chop straw and thresh corn. Those jobs were done by hand after that, so I found myself working like a horse during the day and nursing a sick horse during the night. Sleeping in the stable, I was on hand to help the horse to its feet about every hour.

It was at this time I made a fool of myself. Mrs Rewers was making butter and I was on look out in the loft. I saw a figure in a long cape leave the village and come towards the farm. Mrs Rewers was expecting a woman friend and I assumed it would be her. I went down to tell Mrs Rewers and saw Mroz prick up his ears. I reassured him in my newly learnt language and told him to keep quiet. Suddenly Mroz went mad, breaking the chain and almost leaping the fence. A German policeman in a long coat was about four hundred yards away. I grabbed a bucket and opened the door of the sty where the two spare pigs were kept. Seeing the bucket, they followed me out of the back gate and Jolanta and Slawek drove them into the fields. There was no time to do anything else. I had to dive through the dog kennel into my hide-out. I lay there wondering and hoping Mrs Rewers had managed to get the butter-churn out of the way. When Mroz stopped barking, I knew the German had gone, but I hesitated at coming out, somehow I felt ashamed. Eventually Wojciech called me and I went out. His face was white with rage. I expected a torrent of abuse, but he looked at me disdainfully and uttered two words in Polish, *'glupi osiol'* (stupid donkey). He never spoke another word all day, neither did Mrs Rewers. I knew the German had found something, but I daren't ask what.

I was thankful to go to my hole in the straw that night. I thought of leaving, but where would I go, with the temperature at twenty below zero?

Next morning the atmosphere had not changed, I ate my breakfast in silence, feeling I was about to choke. I did what work I thought wanted doing and then sat in the stable pondering what to do. Mrs Rewers came into the stable and put her arm round my shoulder. 'It could have been worse Colin, he could have caught you,' and she sobbed her heart out. The ice was broken and after a while, I found out what had happened.

Mrs Rewers hid the butter, but instead of passing the churn to me in the hide-out, decided to scald it out and hide it in the house, thinking the German would be checking the stock or something outside.

The purpose of his visit was that someone had mentioned Wojciech had a full volume of encyclopaedias and they were very rare in Poland. He searched the house from top to bottom. He found the butter-churn, but not the books. After dinner, Wojciech jumped up and said, 'Come Colin, you and I can make a new butter-churn, but we couldn't write those books.'

It took three days and a few cut fingers, but we made it, much to Mrs Rewers' delight. After that, Wojciech showed me how to make wooden soles for sandals and boots. He said, 'You are only a stupid donkey when it comes to recognising Germans.'

Alex was getting very restless, and he would slip out of Piotr's house to have a walk. He thought, since he could speak German and if anyone stopped him, he could bluff his way out. The danger was the Polish neighbours; strangers were rare and they began to wonder who he was.

One morning, Piotr arrived with his two horses hitched to the wagon, and with him his cousin Yula, along with Alex and Bomber. I thought it was a social visit, but we spent the whole day threshing corn and chopping straw. It solved Wojciech's horse problem and cured Alex's boredom.

This was the first time I'd seen a group of Polish people work. They worked hard, but with a sense of humour. Most of the horseplay was between Alex and Yula. She was a young woman about thirty years old, and her husband taken for forced labour in Germany. The Germans had taken possession of her farm and meanwhile she stayed with Piotr.

During the break for coffee, Alex made a few attempts to tie Yula in a bale of straw, but she was too strong for him. The climax came when work started again. Yula collected straw for a bale, and when she'd enough, she grabbed hold of Alex and tied him in the bale. What happened next was unbelievable. She stuck a hayfork in the bale and hoisted it and Alex as well, onto the top of the stack. A subdued Alex slid down the ladder to a chorus of laughter.

At the end of the day, we all had supper together and then we talked. Of course, everyone was told how I'd mistaken a German policeman for an old woman.

During the conversation, Bomber asked why the dog was named Mroz, which means 'frost' in English. Piotr explained: Wojciech had a very good housedog. Well, actually, it was a bitch and it got loose and disappeared. Sometime later, Slawek was playing in the small plantation near the farm and he ran home and told his mother something was crying in the bushes. She went with him and there in the snow they found the missing dog and five pups. Four pups and the dog had frozen to death. She wrapped the one live puppy in her shawl, brought it home, bottle-fed it and luckily it survived. This was the only one to beat the frost, so they called it Mroz.

Spring wasn't far away and Alex was anxious to leave. Piotr kept asking him to be patient, but I think he realised with or without papers, Alex would soon be gone. It was the first week in March, when Piotr arrived looking very worried. He had a very heated argument with Wojciech. I couldn't follow the gist of their conversation as they spoke too fast. Whatever the argument, Piotr always won.

When he'd gone, Wojciech said, 'Tomorrow you'll have to kill one of the pigs, and I'm not happy about it.'

I could understand that because the pig wasn't ready. Remembering the argument, I asked, 'But, why do you have to kill it so soon?'

'When you want something in this country Colin, you have to pay for it, and you can't pay in money, because that's only paper.'

'Does Piotr want something so much that you have to kill a pig prematurely?'

My question embarrassed him and he walked away. Then he turned and said, 'I shouldn't tell you this, but Piotr wants some papers for you and your friends.'

What remarkable people these Poles were, risking their lives and making sacrifices for us without any thought or hope of repayment.

Early next morning, Mrs Rewers had a huge container, normally used for boiling potatoes, on the stove full of water. She called to me when the water was boiling and I stunned the pig. Wojciech and I had just lifted it onto the bench, when Mroz raised the alarm. Wojciech ran to the fence and shouted back, 'Quick, let's get it in the hide-out.'

What a blessing it wasn't fully-grown or we wouldn't have pushed it through the hole. All Mrs Rewers seemed concerned about was a pail for the blood. The Poles were fond of *kiska*, similar to black pudding, so her parting remark as she passed me the pail was, 'If you spill it Colin, I'll have yours.'

It was difficult to get in the hide-out, let alone kill a pig in there. I was worried the pig would regain its senses and start squealing before I could kill it, but I managed to drag it on top of a sack of corn, so that I could get the pail under it.

I could hear the Germans going backwards and forwards between the barn and the house arguing and shouting at Wojciech. They wanted to know where the rest of the grain was hidden. He had a lot of straw, but not much grain. I listened to Wojciech's tale of a dry summer and a wet autumn. I was in the hide-out for about two hours with a dead pig on one side of me and a pail of blood on the other, until I had the all clear.

Towards the end of March, the uncertainty and inactivity and, on top of that, the Polish food were playing havoc with Alex. He was pleased when Piotr told us that we would be on our way to Ostrolenka the following week.

Ostrolenka, on the Russian border, was our ultimate destination. When I told Wojciech the news, he said he already knew, and to my surprise he said, 'I wish you would change your mind because your troubles won't be over if you get to Russia. That's where they will begin.'

Alex and Bomber visited as usual on Sunday night. When they arrived, I knew there was something wrong. 'Have we had a cancellation?' I asked.

Bomber blurted out, 'They can only get two identity papers and if this idiot thinks I'm staying here, he's got another think coming.'

'Don't get excited Bomber,' I tried to reassure him, 'one of us can go without papers or we adopt the usual practice and cut cards.'

Piotr explained, now they could only get two identity papers, but later on, they would get the other. Wojciech Rewers spoke, Alex and Bomber didn't understand what he was saying, but I did. He wanted Alex and Bomber to go, arguing they were more at risk than I was. I quickly nipped that idea in the bud by fetching the playing-cards belonging to Wojciech.

'Ace high, the one with the lowest card stays.'

I drew a three; you couldn't get much lower than that. The other two both drew a Jack.

'It's such a serious issue. I think it should be the best of three.'

Alex backed me up, for he wanted me to go with him. We cut the cards again. Lucky Alex drew an ace, Bomber a seven and I drew a five, so I had to accept my lot.

Piotr filled in the identity papers. Alex became Alexander Cikorski and Bomber, Jan Rajmond. The both had to put a thumbprint on the paper and Piotr had brought an inkpad for the occasion.

It was the 6th April when they left Dziedzice. My heart sank as I watch them go. Strangely, I wasn't thinking of me staying behind, my thoughts were with them. Would they make it? In addition, if they didn't, would the Germans get out of them where they had stayed? Wojciech must have been thinking on the same lines, for he said, 'I have my doubts Colin. Alex is a very brave man, but he isn't very cautious.'

All that day there was a lot of activity in the village. The German overseer and half a dozen policemen searched every farm building. We wondered if they'd been informed about Alex and Bomber. Oddly enough, they never visited to Wojciech's farm, but that was no comfort because then we began to wonder why. Wojciech made me laugh by saying, 'If they come we worry, if they don't come we worry.'

As dawn broke next morning, there was pandemonium in the village. A fleet of trucks parked on the road while soldiers and policemen dashed from house to house. Wojciech went down to find out what was happening. He returned ashen faced, and as he entered the yard, he snapped out a command. I didn't understand, but everyone else did. They ran indoors and in two minutes were outside again wearing warm coats. Mrs Rewers had a basket with bread, butter and a large jug of black coffee.

'Come Colin,' they shouted and hurried out of the back gate to the plantation. Wojciech told us what was happening in the village of Dziedzice. Soldiers and police went to every house simultaneously, so that no one could escape. The captives were loaded into waiting trucks and taken to labour camps in Germany. I thought of Alex and Bomber. If they'd stayed another day, they would also be captives, and Piotr shot without question.

About midday, Wojciech went scouting to see what was happening. When he returned, he told us the Germans had moved into the empty farms around the village and the soldiers and police had gone. We returned to Wojciech's farm and carried on working, the danger had passed for the time being. Wojciech said it was because his farm was so isolated that the Germans didn't take possession. There was an air of dejection about the farm. Alex and Bomber had gone. Piotr and the whole village had gone. Before, we could look down to the village and know our friends were there, but now it was an enemy camp.

Wojciech listened to the news from London. It was on the cards that Germany would attack Russia during the summer, but I hoped to be gone by then.

It was now warm enough to sleep in the barn and all the manure had to be loaded and carted to the fields; my job was to load it in the yard. Wojciech wouldn't risk me going in the fields. Working from dawn to dusk, I was too tired to think. It was when the work slackened off, I began to think and get restless.

Impulsively I announced that I had decided to leave the following week. It brought a lump to my throat when I realised how attached the family had become. Mrs Rewers and the children were in tears. Later that afternoon, Wojciech shouted to me, 'Come Colin, we're going for a walk.' This was the first time I'd been outside of the farm in six months, so he obviously had something on his mind that he didn't want his family to hear.

Once in the fields he came quickly to the point. 'If you imagine your troubles are over if you reach Russia, you are mistaken; the Russians never help anyone unless they can make something out of it.'

He was such a genuine man and thought he was giving me good advice, so I put my side of the picture to him. I told him I was very grateful for all he'd done for me, but I'd not escaped from a prison camp to hide in Poland. I owed it to myself and my wife to try to return home; and getting to Russia seemed my only hope.

He put his hand on my shoulder and said, 'I don't agree with you going, but I admire you for it, and we shall help you all we can, and that includes getting you identity papers.' As we walked back to the farm, he pointed to the countryside. 'It would be difficult to find a hiding place out there, wouldn't it?' I had to admit that, and he went on. 'Imagine those green fields filled with corn, waist high. Wouldn't it be easier to hide then? I've promised to get papers for you, now promise me you'll wait until the corn is waist high before you go.'

'How long will that take?'

'Six to eight weeks, depending on the weather,' he laughed. 'Go and stand in the corn every morning and when it reaches your waist, it's time to go.'

One evening Wojciech turned to me and said, 'I think we'd better decide on a name to put on your papers.'

'Let's get the papers first.'

He went to the cupboard and brought out a piece of thin, flimsy paper, it was a blank identity paper. It had the German stamp mark and an impressive looking signature on it. The Christian name needed no thinking about: it had to be Stefan. The first night at Rewers' farm, Slawek had called me Stefan and the name had stuck. I didn't know many Polish names and none that I could spell. My eyes rested on a cocoa tin on the kitchen shelf with the name *'Wysocki'* printed on it.

'That's it,' I said and wrote it on the paper. What a laugh when they asked me to pronounce it and I said, *'Vysoki.'*

'It should be pronounced *Vysotski,'* Wojciech told me.

In the space where it said, 'What language do you speak in the house?' Wojciech told me to write, *'Nie mowe,'* which means deaf and dumb. I couldn't put Polish - by now I had some understanding of the language but no one would believe I was a native Polish speaker when I couldn't even pronounce my own name. My thumbprint completed the form.

I had to practice acting deaf and dumb. Wojciech would say to me in the morning, 'You are deaf and dumb until supper time.'

The dumb part wasn't difficult; I'd plenty of practice at that when I'd first arrived at the Rewers' farm. Acting deaf was the problem. It wasn't just ignoring sounds that were difficult, but not showing signs that you could hear.

Wojciech occasionally crept up behind me while I worked and spoke to me, then he would say, 'You turned your head,' or 'you lifted your head.' I had to be in a world of my own and yet constantly alert. I suggested just being dumb, but he said he'd never known anyone being dumb without being deaf.

One night after supper Wojciech asked, 'How do you fancy a trial run to Slupca tomorrow?' Slupca was the market town and once a week, Wojciech and his wife took produce to sell, some legally and some not.

Early next morning we loaded the cart and the pair set off. I took a short cut across the fields and waited for them by the roadside. I sat in the back of the cart and we agreed if stopped, they would say I'd begged a lift and they didn't know me.

When we were doing anything illegal on the farm, Wojciech would be serious and tense. I wondered if his light-heartedness was to give me confidence. As we drove along, he named what the charge and sentence would be.

'Now that sack of rye to be milled is alright, I've got coupons for that, but somewhere among the rye is a radio battery for the miller to charge; they would shoot me for that. For helping an escaped POW, shot without a trial. Then there is the piece of pork and a kilo of butter; that would be a thousand zloty fine and six months in prison. You are a lucky man Stefan. You would go back to a prison camp and I'd be shot twice, fined a thousand zloty and a prison sentence.'

When we neared Slupca, I jumped off the cart and Wojciech carried on to the mill. Once in Slupca, I felt self-conscious and wondered if I looked any different from anyone else in the crowd. It was a long day walking aimlessly around. I had a sandwich in my pocket, but after I'd eaten it, I realised I'd not catered for my thirst. A number of men were drinking bottles of beer in a shop, and I was tempted to try my sign language out, then I remembered I'd no money. Eventually, the farmers started moving out of town and I saw Wojciech preparing to leave. I walked along the road we had travelled that morning and soon he caught up with me. As I jumped on the cart he asked, 'How do you feel now you are a Polish citizen?'

'Damn dry!' I replied. 'Thanks for turning me loose without a penny in my pocket.'

The day before I left the Rewers' farm was a day of tears and laughter. As we ate breakfast, Mrs Rewers said, 'This is the last day you'll have with us and we won't know if you are dead or alive.' That started the tears flowing. It broke the spell when Wojciech fetched a jam jar and some sealing wax. His wife asked him what he was going to do and he replied, 'We are going to bury Colin Marshall.'

I'd given Wojciech two photographs of my wife and me. On the back of one were the names and addresses of Alex, Bomber and Jim Smart. After the war, Wojciech was to send the photographs, together with a letter I'd written, to my wife. We placed these in the jar and sealed them with sealing wax. Wojciech led the cortege to where he'd dug a hole in the ground outside the back gate. After the burial of the jar, Wojciech led us back to the house to drink a toast to Stefan Wysocki – *nie mowe*.

The Fic Family

E arly next morning I was on my way bound for, by the grace of God, a place called Ostrolenka on the River Bug next to the Russian border.

It was three miles to the main Poznan to Warsaw road. When I reached it without incident, I felt very confident. I lost a lot of that confidence shortly after, under a hail of blows from a policeman's stick. In between the blows, he repeated that something was *verboten*, but with deaf and dumb papers in my pocket, I couldn't ask him to explain. I had repeat treatment a little later so I decided to quit the main road and take a second-class road, even though it was a lot further to travel. I'd studied the map of Poland for the past six months and knew both routes off by heart. I knew I had to make for Lad, where there was a bridge over the River Warta. If there were guards on the bridge, I'd soon find out if my papers were in order.

When I reached the bridge, three men and a woman were having an argument with a guard. He laid down the law that no more than two Poles could walk together at any time; they were trying to explain the reason the four were together. It was because he'd detained the first two and the other two had just caught up. The argument ended when the guard swiped one of them across the face and then waved them to go. I joined them, expecting him to call me back, but he didn't. The guard at the other end of the bridge pointed to a path through the meadow by the river. Again, he said something was *verboten* but he spoke so fast, I was no wiser. I hurried on ahead of the others, I felt safer without company and the path was easy to follow. When I reached the road again, I realised the guard had done me a good turn. I'd cut a corner and by-passed the small town of Zagorow. The next place was Trabczyn, which consisted of just two cottages and a farm. Soon I arrived at a large building with a notice board. My stride quickened as I read 'District Police Headquarters'. I breathed a sigh of relief when I was clear of that place; one policeman was too many, I didn't fancy meeting a squad of them.

At a fork in the road, a signpost pointed the way to Konin, but that would have taken me back on to the main road. Two figures on horseback, trotting down the road from Konin, caused me to hurry along the other road. Wojciech had warned me, 'It's the SS if they are mounted and they are the worst of all.'

The road had deteriorated into little more than a cart track of sand, and with the sun beating down on my head, it felt like the Sahara desert. Five miles later and I felt all in. My time on the farm had not prepared me for a hard slog like this. The road improved as I reached the next village. A sign in German gave the name of the village of Trustdorfebut and underneath the Polish name of Modlibogowice.

As I passed the first house, an old lady stood by the gate, a black shawl round her shoulders. I decided to ask her for a drink. My sign language worked, I soon made her understand. She invited me into the cottage to rest and gave me a glass of cold black coffee. I felt such a fraud as she carried on talking to me and I just stared at her as if I'd not heard a word. In the end, she started using signs to ask if I wanted something to eat. When I nodded my head, she put on her shawl and beckoned me to follow.

After going through the village, she turned on to a side road that led up to a farm. The farmer, his wife, four daughters and two sons met us at the gate, all interested to know about me. All their questions remained unanswered as I feigned to be deaf and dumb. In the end, the farmer pulled an identity paper from his pocket and pointed to me. I gave him my identity paper and they crowded round to read it. 'Nie mowe', they exclaimed and looked at me as if I was a freak of nature.

The old lady interrupted them by saying, 'I thought you would give him some dinner as I haven't a thing in the house.' That brought a swift reaction. I was ushered into the house. The frying pan was on the stove and in no time, I was sitting down to fried bread with scrambled eggs, followed by pancakes with fruit juice. After dinner, the farmer insisted on showing me round his farm. I wanted to be on my way, but I just couldn't walk off without showing a little courtesy. He made straight for the stables to show me his two horses. By the look on his face, they were his pride and joy. What a difference to the old nag who had been my bedmate during the winter. That brought my mind back to my immediate problem; what was *verboten*? I looked across the yard. We were alone in the stable. I decided to take a chance.

I said to him in Polish, 'The German police keep driving me off the road, telling me something is *verboten*. What is forbidden?'

His face went white as he asked, 'Who the Devil are you?'

'I'm an Englishman. I've escaped from a POW camp and I'm on my way to Russia. That's why I want to know what is forbidden.'

Perhaps I was foolish telling him who I was, but I couldn't have papers stating deaf and dumb and then suddenly ask him a question, without some explanation.

He told me the Germans were preparing to attack Russia, and it was forbidden for the Poles to be on the main roads while the transports were going though. As we walked round the rest of the farm, he was deep in thought. I was beginning to wish I were a mind-reader when he stopped suddenly and asked if I'd like to stay with him and his family. Without waiting for me to answer, he went on to tell me his eldest son had died, his manservant taken for forced labour and consequently, he had no man to help him on the farm. If I worked for him, he would take the risk of sheltering me. He seemed disappointed when I declined his offer and asked me to remember, if I failed to reach Russia and if I could get back, the offer would still stand. I took leave of Franc Fic after asking him not to tell anyone, not even his family, who I was.

I pressed on until dusk, before finding shelter for the night. I begged supper and a bed in a barn without any trouble. Early the following morning and I'd not gone very far, when I met a policeman on a cycle. He waved me off the road so hard with his stick, he nearly fell off. I turned into the field and hurried on. When I thought the coast was clear, I returned to the road. A little later, I heard a string of swear words in German, and turned to see the same policeman behind me. He didn't wave his stick this time, but crashed it across my ear. For a moment, I almost forgot I was deaf and dumb. As I made myself scarce, I realised it would be safer to give the police a wider berth.

It was very confusing following the minor roads, some of them like cart tracks. Twice, I came to a dead end and had to retrace my steps. The second time, I found myself in a farmyard and since it looked quite a large farm, I quickly turned back. I could have bet my life on it belonging to a German.

A woman walked through a gate on to the road, just ahead of me. I raised my cap and went to walk on by, but she stepped in front of me and asked why I'd been to the farm. She spoke in Polish, but I was sure she was German, so it was only half-heartedly I motioned I wanted something to eat. It was then that she saw the side of my face, which by this time was very swollen. She spoke so fast, all I could understand was *Matka Jezusa* (Mother of Jesus), so at least she was a Christian.

She led me back to the house, firing questions as we went. How? Where? When? I felt so stupid trying to tell her by signs, so finally I gave up. As I ate the bread and milk she gave me, she put some dried herbs in a pan of boiling water and mulched them. I left the farm with a poultice of herbs, held in place with strips of white cloth covering one side of my face. I wanted to take it off, but I couldn't hurt the lady's feelings. I decided to leave it on until I reached the road, but then the pain started to ease and so I left it on, much to the amazement of some passers-by.

On the second night after leaving the Rewers' farm, I slept in a barn, but strangely enough, I had company. The whole family were sleeping there as well, as it was too hot in the house. Before I dropped off to sleep, I wondered where I was. I reckoned somewhere between Turek and Keczyca, according to the map in my memory. Tomorrow I'd risk staying on the main road, so that I could see a signpost to get my bearings.

Next morning I took the dressing off my face because it was attracting too much attention. That farmer's wife knew her herbs, because all the pain had gone.

Two things disturbed me as I walked along the road. No one stopped me, and I passed two policemen and secondly, the sun was continually in the wrong place. My fears were confirmed when I eventually saw a signpost, which said: *Kalisz 8 kilometres*. I abruptly turned left; I didn't need a map to tell me I was too far south.

The date was Sunday 22nd June 1941 when I passed through Lodz, and I overheard a farmer telling his wife that Germany had invaded Russia. As I travelled the road from Lodz to Warsaw, I wondered how the Russians would cope. Would my journey be in vain?

Over supper that night in a labourer's cottage, I listened while he told me how the Russians were going to push the Germans back over the River Warte. He must have forgotten that I'd begged my supper by making signs. Next morning, I resumed my journey with mixed feelings. If only I could find out what was happening.

I passed through the small town of Glowno. A group of men stood talking; this was unusual as the Germans banned it. One of them had a newspaper. As I drew close, I could see the headlines: *German tanks tear through Russia*. It was then I decided to return to Fic's farm.

Franc Fic was overjoyed to see me. The rest of the family's feelings varied from suspicion, amazement and fear, especially when Mrs Fic broke down and cried, and I turned to Fic and said in Polish. 'I don't want to upset your wife. I think I'd better leave.'

Mrs Fic gasped, 'He can talk!' Fic had kept his word; his family thought I was deaf and dumb.

Later on after supper, they had another shock when Fic told them who I was, and that he'd asked me to stay and work for him. He also made the family understand that everyone outside the family must believe I was deaf and dumb. I realised they were taking a great risk. I told them, in less than perfect Polish, that I'd only stay if they all agreed.

Mrs Fic gave the lead and she put her arm round me saying, 'What we have, you share.'

She told me her eldest daughter Sally and her husband were both safe and well working in France, but there was little hope of them returning home until the war ended.

The eldest daughter at home was Irena. She was twenty-three and her fiancé was in Germany, taken for forced labour.

Next was Gene, almost twenty-one and courting a man quite a lot older than her, Mietek Potrolczak. He was a clerk in the Area Council Offices in Konin. His brother Max was a clerk in the local council offices.

Then there was Kaszmira, seventeen, with hair like burnished copper and vitality running out of her ears. She certainly set my alarm bells ringing, especially when they said she was unattached.

Baszka came next; she was eleven years old, talked like a machine gun, a born comic and a mimic.

The oldest boy was Tadeusz; he was eight and the trouble spot of the family.

Feliks, the youngest, was five and the apple of everyone's eye.

When the introductions were over, I decided to give them my credentials; perhaps it would stop any misunderstandings. I told them I was happily married. In addition, I was a poor man, a coal miner, so there was no chance of any reward for helping me.

The next few days I kept a low profile. Fic told me he'd invited his future son-in-law, Mietek, and his brother to visit the following Sunday to talk things over. Mietek couldn't wait until Sunday; he arrived the same night.

When I first saw him, I thought he was a German. He was a big man, a bit on the podgy side, and his head clean-shaven. He laughed it off by saying he shaved his head to disguise his age. When he left, he promised to bring his brother Max, on Sunday. He felt sure that between them, they could help me.

I kept myself busy stitching the horse's harness and doing chores around the farm; but a couple of things worried me. The water for the stock and for the house had to be carried from the neighbour's well, which was far too shallow to be healthy. The well in Fic's yard was a mystery. The two uprights that held a long pole fixed to the top, which acted as a fulcrum to lift the bucket, seemed in good order, but the bucket hung unused and rusted. Looking down the well, there were only feathers and leaves, but no one seemed to be prepared to say why no one used it.

In addition, the sleeping arrangements weren't very satisfactory. The farmhouse consisted of two large rooms and a small kitchen. One room was a dining-cum-bedroom, with two beds; the other was a sitting room-cum-bedroom, with two beds. The first night, I slept in a bed with the two boys, in the same room as Fic and his wife. Next morning I started looking round for a change of sleeping quarters.

The barn was twice as large as Rewers', but there was very little straw and that was only fit to bed down cattle. The other building consisted of the stable, cowshed, a corn store, a pigsty and finally the chickenhouse. The upper storey of this building was the hay store, but it was the corn store beneath that caught my eye. Under German occupation, a corn store wasn't required. Fic seemed pleased when I suggested I could sleep there. He even agreed to me cutting a trapdoor into the hay store above. I found two bed ends in the barn, and with some spare timber, I soon made a bed. It felt good that night, sleeping in a bed of my own, in my own room.

Sunday in Poland was a day for visiting, and since the gossips had spread it around there was a stranger at Fic's, we had a flood of visitors. I began to realise what acting deaf and dumb was all about. On the journey from Rewers' farm, I'd been a passing ship, moving on each day. As the day wore on, I began to feel like the star attraction in a peep show.

Fic told all the visitors that I was his sister's son, and my parents taken for forced labour in Germany. The Germans hadn't taken me because I was deaf and dumb, so my mother had given me a note, and asked friends to see that I reached Franc Fic at Modlibogowice.

That day was the beginning of weeks of hell as I struggled to keep up the pretence. I thought of the game we played at school – O'Grady says do something and you did it, if they didn't say O'Grady, you didn't do it. Now O'Grady says, 'Keep your mouth shut,' and this was for real because there were more lives at stake than just mine.

The last two visitors, Mietek and Max, were very welcome. We all laughed when they told us how their sister, who had visited Fic's during the afternoon, had described me as, 'clean, smart and with bold eyes that seemed to look right through you. He doesn't hear a thing, but he laughs when everyone else does. At times he looked so deep in thought; perhaps he was thinking of his parents.'

The story Fic gave out about my identity appeared to be accepted. After supper, when it was certain there would be no more visitors, they discussed how best they could help me. Max copied the details off my identity paper, so that he could then copy them onto the register at the council office. When they left, I felt sick with apprehension at Mietek's parting remark. 'We can help you, but it all depends on how well you play your part. If you fail, we shall all go against the wall.'

That gave me a sleepless night, but it strengthened my resolve. I'd play the part no matter what happened.

The next morning I surprised Fic. I'd fed and groomed the horses before he woke. He asked why I was up so early. I didn't tell him I couldn't sleep for worrying. I just said, 'If I'm staying here, I've got to earn my keep.'

After breakfast, he fetched two scythes from the shed and handed one to me. Then he began to sharpen his with a large round stone. He criss-crossed the stone down the blade, as I'd seen the butcher at home sharpen knives. He gave me the stone and I noticed the whole family had turned out to watch the performance. It was so amusing to them that I couldn't sharpen a scythe. It was only after eight-year-old Tadeusz gave me a demonstration that I began to get the hang of it; then I became too confident and cut my finger.

Later, after the dew had dried, we went down to the meadows. Fic explained he wanted me to learn to use a scythe as the corn was ripening, and the corn harvest was the busiest time on the farm. I didn't get much in the way of instruction before a man walked down the meadow.

Fic nodded in his direction and muttered, 'He's curious, so be on your guard.' I carried on trying to master the art of scything, while Fic answered the curious gentleman's questions. He thought it strange I couldn't use a scythe, until Fic explained I could do anything round the farm, but my mother had been possessive and not allowed me out in the fields. He interrupted Fic to voice his approval of my performance.

I just carried on scything and he said to Fic, 'Doesn't he hear anything at all?'

What a clever answer Fic gave: 'Sometimes I think he has heard me and then I realise he anticipates what I was going to do.'

The man was all ears as Fic explained, 'This morning when we left the house, I said to him, "We'll feed the horses" and he went straight to the barn for the feed, but when I went to the door and shouted, "only half a skip this morning," he still brought a full one.'

After he'd taken his leave, I asked Fic why he'd made up that story. He said, 'In a village, convince one and you convince ninety five percent. But you still have to watch the other five percent.'

Having mastered the art of using a scythe, I was able to turn my mind to other things. I explained to Fic the set up at Rewers' farm. How it was possible to move unseen through different parts of the buildings. He gave me a free hand, providing I didn't attract the attention of the Germans. It wasn't an elaborate system like Rewers', but it would serve its purpose.

My next problem was the water situation. I felt sick every time I fetched a bucket of water from the shallow well in the neighbour's yard. Try as I would, I couldn't get an explanation as to why they didn't use their own well until one morning when I decided to clean it out. Having fastened another bucket to the pole in place of the old rusty one, I started baling out the water. Irena ran out of the house, her face ashen.

'Don't do it Stefan,' she pleaded. 'The well is cursed, it belongs to the Devil.' I thought to myself, if the one next door belongs to the Lord, then I'd rather drink with the Devil. I had to find out what this curse was, but I realised the open farmyard was no place for a dumb man to be asking questions, so I made for the house.

Eventually, although it was very distressing for her, Irena told me the whole story. Just before the war began, the next-door neighbour died and his two sons couldn't agree who should have the smallholding, as it wasn't large enough to share. They went to the court in Konin to sort it out and Fic lent them his horse and cart for the journey. The outcome was that the married brother was to have the smallholding, but he was to pay a certain sum to the court each month for the other brother. This caused more bitterness because it was hard to live off such a small place without having to pay a debt.

It was dark when the two brothers returned home from Konin and as they un-harnessed the horse, Irena, who had gone to the toilet across the yard, heard them quarrelling. She was afraid and decided to wait until they'd gone. She heard a thud and a splash and then silence. When she came out of the toilet, there was no one there. She told her father what she'd heard. Next morning the wife of the brother visited to say that her brother-in-law had gone away. The thud and the splash flashed across Irena's mind and she dashed across the yard to the well. The water was crystal clear and lying in a jack-knife position with his face looking upwards was the missing brother. Irena shuddered as she recalled the incident, so I hurriedly asked her what had happened to the married brother. Her face changed, there was a determined look on her face and she spoke with bitterness saying how she'd had to go in the witness box, and how they'd tried to make her admit she'd imagined the argument, thud and splash.

'It may sound strange to you,' she said, 'but the Church here is as strong as the law. The priest spoke up for him because the married brother gave more than he could afford to the Church. If I hadn't insisted on what I had overheard, he would have got off. As it was, he only got six months in prison. Yes, six months for murder, Stefan. In addition, if he survives the war, he will come back. Don't touch that well; there's a curse on it,' she pleaded.

It was hard to disappoint her, but I explained I may have to stay with them one or two more years, and I wasn't going to drink dirty water from the well next door. As for the curse, that should be on the house next door. I went out and started emptying the well, much to the dismay of the whole family, except for the two young boys. No one spoke to me for the rest of the day as I toiled. Fortunately it was the dry season, or the water would have run back as fast as I baled it out. When I reached the silt, I had to go down the ladder to fill the bucket and then climb back up to the top to haul the bucket out. If only one member of the family had helped, it would have taken half the time. I carried on working as it grew dusk. If I'd stopped, the water would fill up again. By the light of a lantern, I reached a bed of pebbles at the bottom of the well; at last, I'd succeeded.

The last few minutes brought a little humour to the situation. As I climbed the ladder for the last time with the lantern in my hand, my shoulder caught the pole attached to the bucket by a short chain. The chain rattled and I heard a piercing scream. I hurried up the remaining steps of the ladder in time to see the vague figure of someone running down the drive. All the family came out to see what had happened. A little later, the mystery was solved when half a dozen villagers, together with the woman next door, arrived to investigate the ghost with a lantern, appearing from the well.

Next morning I went to view the results of my labour. The well was half-full of crystal clear water, but no way could I convince the rest of the family to drink it. It was a matter of convincing Irena. More and more I began to realise who was the ruling force in that house.

By then I'd become well known in the village. Although I couldn't greet people in the traditional way, I just raised my cap. This was a great help when the corn harvest started. The novelty of scrutinising me had worn off, although I still had to be on my guard, the pressure wasn't so great. I was acquiring a way of closing my mind to what was said around me but still being alert.

The first day of the harvest was on a neighbouring farm. There where twenty men with scythes, each accompanied by a woman who followed him and tied the corn in sheaths as he cut. A cane bow on the handle of the scythe near the blade made it possible to lay the corn in a straight line, so that the women could gather it more easily. Irena decided to accompany me as she was more capable of dealing with any inquisitors, but she very soon regretted that decision. When Fic taught me to use the scythe, he taught me to take a wide sweep, taking as much as possible with each sweep. This was different, the others were taking short sweeps, I was taking long ones and Irena was working twice as hard as the other women were. Once up the field was enough. She raised a laugh by doing a bit of sign language herself. She put her fist in my face and then pointed out what I was cutting, opposed to the others. I learnt my lesson, especially later when I found myself wondering if I'd last out the day. Hour after hour, swinging that scythe... and I thought pit work was hard. At the end of the day, someone started scraping on a two stringed fiddle and everyone danced like mad. Me? Well I dragged my weary body back home to bed.

The following day it was a different farm. Irena explained how the system worked. When the corn was ready, every farmer put their name into a hat and when drawn out, the people all congregated at that farm and so everyone had their turn. Everyone regarded it as a jolly time, but to me it was sweated labour. At the end of the day, some of the farmers gave everyone drinks, not like the vodka that Wojciech Rewers made, just a concoction of methylated spirits and fruit juice. Some of them would have liked to get me drunk for the fun of it, but I was on my guard.

There was one man in the village, who wasn't convinced about my identity. Everyone called him Old Robok. He was certainly old, and he could work, despite the fact that winter or summer he never wore boots, just masses of rags round his feet; he reminded me of a shire horse. He did casual labour round the village, paid for in produce. Old Robok insisted he knew me when I was knee high. Apparently, one of Franc Fic's sisters had a boy called Michael, who was a bit deficient and highly-strung. That boy had been dead for years, but Old Robok wouldn't believe that and always insisted on calling me Michael. He said I was acting deaf and dumb to avoid being taken for forced labour. Whenever he came to Fic's, he watched me like a hawk.

For two weeks, Irena and I'd been out every day to neighbouring farms, and then it was Fic's turn. Chickens had been dressed the previous night ready to feed all the workers. No matter how sparsely one lived, you had to do the harvesters proud. As we all gathered in the field waiting to start work, Baszka, the youngest daughter, ran to us with a message. 'Stefan must take the lead. Father has got to go to Rychwal.'

The practice was, the farmer took the lead cutting his own corn and then he couldn't grumble that others were going too slow. There was laughter all round at that message because everyone knew Fic had taught me to use a scythe only a few weeks before. The man in the meadow had spread the news. I was all right following the pack, but I hadn't a clue what pace to make. I just kept my eye on Irena, when I was leaving her behind I slowed the pace. How enlightening it was to hear them talking about me thinking I couldn't hear them. One loud voice shouted, 'He'll be flat on his back before coffee break.' Another said, 'It's in his blood. All his family are farmers.'

Coffee break came and went without any worry, but I was hanging on before dinner time. Every swing seemed to pull on my empty stomach. Dinner was from midday until two o'clock. It was too hot to work during those hours and I was grateful for the rest. Fic returned from Rychwal and I thought he would take over the lead, but he didn't. The scythe didn't worry me now and I was into the swing, and I felt I could go on forever. Instead, I began to worry about a pain in my foot. It was throbbing as if there was an infection in it, yet I couldn't see anything. What a relief when the day ended. Everyone patted me on the back, but all I wanted to do was rest my foot. They all filed in for supper, but I made straight for my bed in the corn store. After supper, Irena arrived with a lantern; there was no window in the store. At first, I thought she'd brought my supper until I saw a cloth in a jug of water, a bottle of methylated spirit, a penknife and a box of matches.

'What's all that for?' I asked.

She wrung the cloth out and gave it to me. 'Put that in your mouth and bite on it. I'm going to do a painful operation or you are going to lose your foot or your leg.'

She reminded me of my mother as she dipped the knife in the methylated spirit and ran the lighted match down it.

'Before you do anything, I think you had better tell me what's wrong with my foot.'

'It's not your foot. It's here,' she said, pointing in between my toes. 'You've been working in the cornfield barefoot and the stubble has cut the skin and you've hundreds of whiskers of corn packed under the skin.'

She took the cloth from my hand and put it to my mouth saying, 'Bite hard, this is going to be hell.'

The stuff she prised from between my toes was unbelievable. I began to think she was a magician. We packed all the pieces into the empty matchbox, filling it. After bathing my foot in salt water, about the cheapest and only cure in Poland, it felt much better.

Irena didn't want me to work the next day, but when I wrapped my feet in old clothes like Robok, she was satisfied. That was how I finished the harvest and learned my lesson: bare feet and stubble are deadly enemies.

'Now the harvest is finished, what next?' I asked Fic.

'Well there's the winter ploughing, the potatoes need harvesting and the peat digging for the winter, but today you can drive Mother (meaning Mrs Fic) to Konin.'

I can't say I enjoyed that day. There seemed enough German soldiers in Konin to man the Eastern Front. Of course, I had my identity paper and Max had made sure that I was registered, but I couldn't help feeling nervous. It was obvious the whole family had been nervous too by the way they greeted us when we returned home.

The war news was beginning to get on my nerves. It was too one-sided to be wholly true. It occurred to me I could go back to the Rewers and find out some definite news from their radio. I set off on foot for Dziedzice after promising to be back in a few days. It was much easier going back, but I reflected ruefully, the last time I'd travelled this ground I was full of optimism; now it was stalemate.

The welcome at Rewers' was unbelievable, I felt like the Prodigal Son. They couldn't wait to hear what had happened to cause me to return. They had to wait until I paid my respects to Mroz; his welcome was the loudest of all.

Wojciech was amazed that I'd managed to act the part of a deaf and dumb Pole and had held down a job on a farm. He was curious to know all about Fic, also the food situation. My answer to that was they didn't live as well as the Rewers family, but they managed.

Wojciech summed it up by saying, 'You exist within the law; you live outside it.' When I mentioned that Fic had three grown up daughters, Wojciech was very concerned. 'For your own sake Stefan, don't get involved,' he advised.

The radio news wasn't much better than I'd already heard, except that the Germans weren't advancing so fast now. Stalin had ordered the Russians to burn everything as they retreated.

When I told them I was returning the following day, there was a wave of protest, but I'd promised Fic I would return to help store the harvest in the barn.

Before I left, Wojciech and Mrs Rewers told me I could always stay with them if I needed to. They gave me a parcel of meat saying, 'Get rid of it, if it looks like you will be stopped.'

I made the journey back to Modlibogowice without incident and as I walked up the drive with the parcel under my arm, the cry went up, 'He's back!' Later they said that they thought I'd been worked so hard, I'd gone back to Rewers' farm and wouldn't return.

After supper, Fic told me we would be getting the corn in the following day. I was up early and after feeding the horses, I cut some wooden stakes and placed them at an angle against an inside wall of the barn wall, so that when the corn was stacked it would make a narrow tunnel. This made somewhere to hide in case of the dreaded *lapanka*, when rounding up for forced labour took place. After three hard days, the bulk of the corn was collected, but it was credit due to the horses. Fic had good cause to be proud of them. Hence Irena's words, 'His horses first, his children second.'

The family applauded my idea of the hide-out in the barn, but a few weeks later, it brought a great deal of worry to me.

Irena and Gene were working in the fields, Kaszmira and I were chopping straw with a hand machine; I was turning the handle. We heard the sound of horses galloping up the drive; Kaszmira looked out of the door, '*Lapanka!*' she gasped. We dived for the hide-out and only just in time before one of the Germans made straight for the barn.

'Come out you swine,' he shouted, as we heard him rear the ladder upright and climb to the top of the stack of corn. We heard the swish of his stick as he searched the corn looking for us, and then we heard them leave, cursing that they'd not caught anyone.

We were about to come out of hiding when we heard Baszka's voice from the back of the barn saying, 'Don't come out yet, one of them has gone down the meadow. I'll tell you when it is safe to come out.'

'It's a blessing you thought of this,' Kaszmira said as she made herself comfortable, but she was making me uncomfortable as she pressed close to me. As I eased away she asked, 'Why are you afraid?'

'It's not a matter of being afraid,' I answered, 'it's a matter of right and wrong. Your father has given me shelter. How can I let him down by making love to his daughter?'

'Father isn't here, just you and I,' she said and she snuggled closer.

The alarm bells were ringing again. 'You know I'm a married man and have a wife, who is waiting for me in England.'

She interrupted me saying, 'How do you know she isn't making love to someone else?'

'I don't know. It's a matter of trust.' Her closeness was causing me to get hot under the collar; I was only human after all. 'Why should a lovely girl like you bother with a married man? One of these days someone will come along and you will have everything to offer.'

'I know what I've to offer,' she said bitterly as she moved away from me. 'God gave me everything it takes to get a man and then he takes all the men away.'

For the rest of the time, while trapped, there was a sullen silence. It was a relief when we heard Baszka calling us.

I hoped the incident would be forgotten, but it was the beginning of a feud between us, which gradually became worse. I tried to avoid her as much as possible, but there were times when we had to work together.

Once we had to help the widow Mrs Kaczinska and her daughter Zofie to thrash her corn by the ancient method of the flail because she hadn't the machinery installed to drive the threshing machine. She particularly asked for me because she wanted someone to carry the grain up into the loft. Kaszmira was the strongest of the girls, so Fic told her to go with me. Using a flail on your own was bad enough, but five people thrashing a bed of corn, one after the other, was tricky. If anyone got out of sequence, the procedure stopped. To make things worse, Old Robok was facing me and his gaze never left me.

Over coffee he brought up his old subject by saying, 'Michael doesn't fool me. He can hear every word we say.'

Kaszmira answered him, but only to have a dig at me. 'Oh I wish he could hear. Then I'd have a ready-made young man instead of a deaf and dumb donkey.'

That day went down in my memory as the hardest, most tedious and boring day of my life.

All the family were excited at the prospect of going down to the bogs to dig peat, a mixture of work and pleasure. Only a small amount of the best peat was cut into bricks with a spade, and the rest was like mud that had to be barrowed to higher ground and made into bricks with a wooden mould. The highlight of the day was the dinner break, from noon until two o'clock, when everyone would bathe in the miniature lakes that formed from where the peat had been taken. When Irena mentioned that they were all good swimmers, but none as good as Kaszmira, I interrupted by asking to borrow something to wear for swimming. Laughing, she said, 'We don't have bathing costumes, we just undress and dive in.'

The bogs were a wonderful sight. As we drove down the road, you could see a vast expanse of water and willow trees. Here and there stood a stork motionless in the water on one leg or sometimes flying overhead. It was a glorious day; I could understand why they'd been excited. Though the work was hard, it was enjoyable with everyone singing and laughing. At midday, we had sandwiches and milk, cooled by submerging the bottles in the water.

I noticed a small, secluded stretch of water surrounded by trees. It was an ideal place to have a quiet bathe. The sun was scorching and the water was cool. I was really enjoying myself when I saw Kaszmira; she stood on the bank waving. Thinking something had happened and the family wanted me I started to swim towards her. I was about twenty yards from the bank when she let her dress fall from her shoulders and for a split second stood poised on the bank before diving in with hardly a ripple. I wouldn't deny my feelings were of admiration, she was a lovely girl, too lovely to be in the same pool as me, and I made for the bank. She grabbed my foot and pulled me under. I wasn't a bad swimmer on the surface, but I was hopeless under the water. When she let go I surfaced gasping for breath, my troubles were not over. Kaszmira swam underneath me and put her arms and legs round me. I was going down again, when suddenly I became buoyant, she was keeping me afloat.

'How do I feel so close?' she whispered.

'Horrible!' I replied and we started to sink again. I realised I had to play it cool; I was no match for her until I could feel my feet on the bottom of the lake. We drifted closer to the bank and I decided to take a chance. I pulled my knees up then reached for the bottom and pushed towards the bank.

'You English are impossible,' she shouted after me.

Back at work cutting the peat, Kaszmira sang and laughed as if nothing had happened. Somehow, I couldn't switch my happiness on.

'Have you been having trouble with Kaszmira again?' The question came from Irena, as I was bedding the horses down for the night; it took me by surprise.

'I haven't had any trouble with her at all,' I lied.

'Don't lie to me Stefan; I'm trying to help you. When you arrived here we all laughed at the way she tried to impress you. She is at the age when she wants romance. Kaszmira changed the day there was the *lapanka* and you two were alone in the barn. Today you go off on your own to swim, and later I missed Kaszmira. In the afternoon, she was laughing although I could tell it was forced. What happened? It caused you to look so miserable.'

Perhaps it was best to tell Irena without going into details, so I said, 'You were right about the day in the barn. What's worrying me is, Kaszmira doesn't seem to realise I'm a married man and when I leave here, either on my feet or in a box, I want my conscience to be clear. Perhaps it is just romance she wants.' I wanted to change the subject, but she wasn't going to be put off.

'Do you realise there are thousands of young Polish men and women doing forced labour in Germany and from reports that's not all they are doing. I am supposed to be engaged, but my young man couldn't wait to go to Germany. Kaszmira and girls like her feel that when the war ends, most of the men will be either engaged or committed in some other way, and they will be left on the shelf.' She went to the door and then turned round. The colour had gone out of her cheeks. 'Don't have any illusions about Kaszmira; she will go all the way to get a hold on you. So remember if you feel you have to go with someone, ask me.'

The next task I had to learn was ploughing and Gene was anxious to teach me because since the manservant had been taken, she had to help with that task. It was a big disadvantage not being able to speak. The horses were trained to obey a word of command, I had to control them with the reins instead and the horses weren't used to that. I could have done with a spare pair of hands, one on the reins and the other on the plough. They say practice makes perfect, and I was a long way from that, but I was able to manage on my own after a few lessons. Gene was over the moon to be relieved of that task. It was hard for a young woman, especially turning the plough round. Therefore, for the next weeks I was ploughing or picking potatoes. Of the two, I preferred ploughing because I was on my own.

Picking potatoes was a primitive affair. The whole family, plus the widow Zofia and Old Robok, armed with short handled hoes with prongs, each took a row, some stood and others knelt. It was a tedious and back aching job. Two weeks was enough to kill anyone, but not these people, it was their life.

Once the work in the fields was over, it gave me time to think, and that wasn't good for the spirit, a thousand miles from home and with Christmas coming.

Sitting round the fire one Sunday night, I glanced at the clock and it was ten minutes to six. 'Exactly a year ago to the minute, we were climbing over the wire,' I told them. Mietek went and fetched a bottle of vodka, to toast my year of apprenticeship as a Polish farmer.

Early in December, it started to snow and I remembered how cold I'd been the previous winter. I wanted to make a waistcoat out of rabbit skins. Very soon, I had a stack of skins; everyone seemed to be saving them for me. Mietek managed to find some curing powder in Konin and I started to clean the skins, but it was a slow job with a table knife.

When Gene said I wasn't getting on very well, I told her it was because I hadn't a proper knife. 'There's a box of knives in the loft, they belonged to grandfather,' she said. 'Perhaps Father will let you borrow them.'

I found every type of knife you could mention, oiled and wrapped up in a box, which Fic said had been in the loft for more than ten years. Within weeks, I'd made a waistcoat and a pair of fur under-trousers. Now I was prepared for the coldest winter, except for my feet. I then made some new wooden soles for my boots.

A few weeks later, Gene was sitting by the fire with her head in her hands, moaning with raging toothache. 'Why don't you go and have in taken out?' I asked.

Gene lifted her head and said miserably, 'It will be next Tuesday before I can have it out. The Germans have restricted visits to doctors and dentists to one half day a week for the Polish people.'

A certain gentleman, a blacksmith by trade, did have a reputation for extracting teeth with a pair of pliers. It must have been out of desperation when, later that evening, Gene told me to harness the horse, as she wanted to see the blacksmith. Fic told me to take the mare as she was the more docile of the two horses, but he warned me to tie her up securely, as she had a young foal in the stable, and she would be anxious to return home.

It was only three kilometres, and even though it was a bad road, it didn't matter as the sleigh glided over the snow. The blacksmith went to great lengths to explain the risks he was taking, as the Germans would shoot him if they found out. This was the build up to asking an extortionate fee. The price was a small ransom. I was instructed by signs how to stand behind the chair and hold Gene's head back. It was a contest whether he pulled the tooth out before Gene got a stranglehold on his neck with her legs. While Gene was rinsing her mouth with saltwater there was a crash outside. The blacksmith dashed to the door, with me in hot pursuit, just in time to see the horse galloping down the road, taking part of the fence with her.

Fic heard the mare pawing the stable door to get to her foal, her front legs cut and bruised. We arrived home an hour and a half later, almost stiff with cold. Gene had my fur waistcoat wrapped round her face to keep out the cold.

The Poles made a lot of Christmas, even though the churches were closed and the priests interned. I was pleased when the New Year arrived and I wondered what it would bring.

The year 1942 started badly for the Fic family. Early in January, Tadeusz became ill. At first, it was just stomach-ache, but then it became serious. I thought he had appendicitis and told Mrs Fic he ought to see the doctor. Blankets were placed in the cart, and the little boy transported to Rychwal. What a wasted journey. 'Keep him warm and give him this medicine.' It didn't seem to matter that he was just a bundle of skin and bone, with a stomach like a football. I shall never forget the next two weeks of a screaming little boy, pleading for me to blow air onto his burning stomach. Hour after hour, we took turns to nurse him. The one person he kept asking for was missing; his father couldn't face illness. Just before Tadeusz died, Fic arrived to see his son. I held him and I felt him struggle to lift his arm up and clench his fist. 'You wait, you red headed Fic!' he cried. He was bitter. The one person he wanted had neglected him. My bitterness was for the Germans who denied that little boy the treatment he needed.

Mrs Fic was beside herself with grief. This was the second son she'd lost within a few years, but even so, everything was done according to tradition. All the family's clothing coupons went on a new outfit for Tadeusz. I had a nasty shock when I went into the bedroom and there in a coffin, propped up in the corner, was little Tadeusz, dressed as if he was going on a Sunday school outing.

More bad luck, when the foal, tethered with a slip chain on its neck, accidentally got its front leg through the chain. In the struggle to free itself, the chain cut deep into the flesh and Fic was advised to have it destroyed. I asked him to wait a few days to see if there was any chance of saving it. I continually bathed the wound with salt water and fed it by teeming gruel down its throat from a bottle, and after a few days, it began to improve. Eventually the foal began to get better and the only sign of the accident was a terrible scar.

The final blow was when the Germans confiscated Fic's gelding for army service; that horse was Fic's pride and joy. Spring was coming and the farm had only one horse. The mare was strong enough to manage some of the ground, but for the other, Fic had to borrow a horse, but from where? Fic was a proud man, more used to granting favours than asking them. In the end, he thought of asking a neighbour of the widow Kaczinska.

Eduard Rakowski and his sister Helen shared a small farm; neither of them had married, although she had a small son. The farm was a bare existence for them, and their horse was a frame of skin and bone. I was surprised when Fic told me to go and borrow Eduard's horse. 'Me!' I asked disbelievingly.

'Yes, you can make him understand by sign language, but make sure you don't ask Helen, she's stupid.'

I had no trouble making Eduard understand Fic wanted to borrow the horse, but I had some difficulty persuading him that Fic didn't want him as well. Perhaps it was as well he didn't come, because when Fic saw the state of the horse and its harness he went mad. I had to spend an hour grooming the horse and another repairing the harness before I could start work.

I'd not realised how difficult it was ploughing with one good horse and one bad one. I had to alter the pull, so that the mare was doing nearly all the work; even then, Eduard's horse was hardly tightening the traces. Fic told me to give it some whip, but I couldn't. I remembered being half-starved and not able to pull my weight.

The next time we had to borrow Eduard's horse, I suggested we managed with just our mare, but Fic seemed concerned that his neighbours might think he was cruel to overwork his horse. 'Go and borrow Eduard's horse, but don't bring the harness, we will use our own.'

It wasn't my lucky day. Eduard was out and Helen answered the door. I made her understand I wanted to borrow the horse, but when I tried to show her with sign language that I didn't want its harness or clothes she screamed and grabbed a brush and chased me off the farm. What a laugh it caused. She told everyone I went to borrow the horse, and then wanted her to take off her clothes.

The war news, when I walked back to Rewers' farm at Dziedzice, wasn't encouraging. Pearl Harbour had brought Japan and America into the war. The Germans were in Africa, but it was stalemate on the Eastern Front. The Germans had failed to reach Moscow before the winter but apparently, if the Germans took Stalingrad, the Russians would collapse. I didn't believe that. I had a feeling they'd bitten off more than they could chew. Rations were reduced, even for the Germans, which was another good sign.

For six days a week, I was too busy to brood over things. There was so much to do on the farm and if I had any spare time, I made sandals for the family. It was the seventh day that drove me to distraction; apart from feeding the stock, no one worked on Sunday.

Fic was pleased when I suggested taking the horses down to the meadow to graze. The mare was contented enough, but we had to put a rope on the colt's front feet to stop it from running away. In England, the fields are fenced off, but the only fence seen in Poland was the one round the farmyard. When the cattle were in the meadow, someone had to watch them. This was Baszka's job, so when I took the horses, I offered to look after the cattle at the same time. I was well rewarded by the look on her face, as she dashed off to play. What a life she had, minding cattle seven days a week.

In the middle of the meadow was a pond where the cattle drank. A willow tree flourished by its edge. With the help of a broken mirror placed in the tree, I could sit by the pond and have a good view of the whole meadow, though sometimes I doubted the wisdom of this idea, as I sat there thinking and thinking until I thought my head would burst.

On Good Friday, something happened that I'd been dreading since the day I drove Gene to the blacksmith-cum-dentist. I started with toothache. I made up my mind to suffer anything before going to that man, but by the following day, I'd have let him knock it out with a hammer. Irena went with me, although she was worried, she didn't say anything until we were in sight of the smithy, when she put her hand on my arm.

'Remember Stefan, if you utter one word, either in Polish or English, you are finished and all our family.' Then as a further warning she added, 'This place is the biggest gossip shop in the district.'

The blacksmith was only too pleased to oblige, he thoroughly enjoyed showing me what he was going to do. Eventually he got the grips on my tooth. I felt relieved when it moved, then with a crunch the grips slipped. With a string of curses, he informed Irena he'd broken the tooth and worse still, he hadn't the tools to finish the job. I shall never forget the next few days; I thought I'd go mad.

Tuesday was the official dentist day for the Poles in that area. I was in such a state; even Irena was loath to go with me. I was prepared to go on my own rather than suffer any longer, but in the end, Mrs Fic went with me. What a relief when the dentist dropped that tooth in the bowl. He patted me on the back, presumably because I hadn't made a murmur.

The following week a feeling of fear gripped the whole village. A rumour spread that some farms were being taken over by Germans who were retreating from Russia. Mietek confirmed this and he managed to find out the exact date.

The Fic family packed up all their personal belongings ready to move out quickly and hide, to avoid forced labour. Fic asked me if I was going back to Dziedzice, and was surprised when I said I was staying with them.

I told Fic that when Piotr Rewers and most of the farmers from Dziedzice had been taken for forced labour, the district commissioner had visited the farms a few weeks before, no doubt to see if any of their possessions were worth taking for himself. This had happened on every occasion since. The gentleman in question had made a routine visit to two farms in the village, two of the largest and both close together. I told Fic that those two farms would be taken first, but he wouldn't believe me.

They sat up all night and about four o'clock in the morning the dog started barking and they decided it was time to move out.

When Irena knocked on the door of the corn store and asked if I was going with them I said, 'No.'

Within an hour, the village was quiet again. I climbed out of bed, fed the horses, and started to milk the cows. It was seven o'clock when the family returned. My forecast was right; the two farms had been taken. Mrs Fic was so excited. 'Stefan, you must be a witch, you can tell the future,' she said. 'I wish I could, but I can only see the past,' I told her. In my mind, I knew the next farm to be taken in Modlibogowice would be Franc Fic's, but I thought it best to say nothing.

Living With Danger

The news was so conflicting; on one hand, the Germans were preparing a two-pronged attack, one on Stalingrad and the other on the Caucasus to cut off the Russian oil. The other report was that the Russians were preparing to counter-attack from Stalingrad, southeast toward Rumania.

Towards the end of April, I made a trip to Rewers' farm. Just before I left, Fic asked me if Rewers would be able to get some corn milled for him. The Germans had cut the bread ration again and things were very difficult, but I was rather concerned because I felt Rewers had done enough for me.

It was like a tonic talking to Wojciech Rewers, we seemed to be on the same wavelength. Everyone else seemed gloomy because the Germans had taken all the Balkans and Greece and then gone into Africa. We agreed that the more territory Hitler took, the more soldiers he would need to guard it.

Wojciech told me he believed the Germans suspected him of having a radio. They'd recently searched the farm a couple of times. He seemed very tense when he listened to the news that day; he had everyone on lookout.

As I was getting ready to leave the following day, I told him my fears about Fic losing his farm, and as he shook my hand he said, 'If that happens Stefan, come back here.' Then he asked, 'By the way, how are the new ration cuts affecting you?'

I wouldn't have mentioned it, if he hadn't asked. 'Fic isn't as enterprising as you Wojciech. Bread is out of the question now; we're living on potato cakes. We have some corn, but we can't get it milled.'

It brought a lump to my throat, as I thought what this man would do for me, as he started giving me instructions.

'Next Wednesday leave Franc Fic's farm at Modlibogowice at six o'clock in the morning. Before you leave, put a hundredweight of corn in a bale of straw, and use it as a seat in the wagon and I'll get it made into flour for you. When you arrive here, we will be looking out for you. If there is washing on the line, it's safe. If not, drive on towards the village and Jolanta will be waiting there. Remember, if it's washday, come and help us.'

Mroz interrupted the conversation with his barking. Wojciech dashed upstairs to the loft. He was back in seconds shouting, 'German police from all directions!'

I scrambled through the dog kennel into the hide-out, when Mrs Rewers shouted, 'Here take this!' It was a whole ham joint and butter wrapped in a towel. From what Wojciech had said, the Germans were looking for something more than ham and butter, but it was better to be sure.

Four German policemen strode into the farmyard. 'We know you have a radio. If you hand it over, that will be the end of it. If you don't hand it over and we find it, you will pay the penalty,' one of them shouted.

There seemed to be a ring of defiance in Wojciech's voice as he said, 'I don't have a radio or any need for one, so I've no penalty to pay.'

As they questioned Jolanta and Slawek, a wagon drove into the yard and a group of Polish men jumped out. They unloaded picks and shovels from the back of the wagon, and under German supervision dug up every inch of the yard.

In the centre of the yard was the old disused cog-wheel machine, that years before had been used to chop straw. The machine was held firmly in the ground with stones and cement. As they dug round, I dreaded to think what would happen if they noticed that one of the stones was loose.

When it became obvious their work had been in vain, the policeman in charge went up to Wojciech and struck him across the face. 'Where have you hidden the radio?' he demanded in anger and frustration.

I thought Wojciech was going to retaliate, but he controlled himself and replied, 'Whoever told you I'd a radio should have told you where it was hidden.'

He shook his fist at Wojciech saying, 'If we find you have a radio or circulate false news, you will pay for it with your life.'

When Wojciech was sure they'd left, he called to me. 'Come and look what the swine have done.'

The farmyard looked like a ploughed field. By the time we'd had a meal and then levelled the yard, it was too late for me to go back to Fic's farm.

As we sat talking that night, I remarked, 'I should imagine you will stop using the radio now.'

His face set as he replied, 'That radio is the one thing that gives me hope. I've six friends,' he went on as if talking to himself, 'to each one I give the news. Now I find one has a loose tongue; therefore I can't trust any of them.'

When I left next morning he reminded me again of the plan for the following Wednesday. 'Remember if it's washday, come and help us.'

Fic was pleased when I told him of the arrangements for milling some flour, but not Irena, she was furious. 'Father, why don't you ask your own relations in the forest, they have a mill there?' she asked.

I was surprised when she said she was going with me to Rewers' farm. 'I thought you didn't approve of the arrangements,' I said.

'I don't!' she snapped, 'but I'm anxious to see this marvellous family, to see if they are real.'

The washing on the line was visible long before we arrived. We didn't stay long at the farm. Curious people would soon want to know why a wagon had come all the way from Modlibogowice. However, we didn't leave before Mrs Rewers had a talk with Irena.

On our way back, Irena told me Mrs Rewers wanted to know about the relationship between us. She said, 'Obviously you've talked about me and she had her suspicions.'

'What did you tell her?'

'I knew that you were married and loved your wife and I was prepared to do anything to help you go back safe. You know she is a very shrewd woman and she did a lot of questioning, so I told her straight. If you had not been married, things would have been different.'

We made the journey back without any mishap, and found the whole family waiting anxiously for our return.

It was June and nearly a year since I first called at Franc Fic's farm. Fic took me with him to the barbers in Rychwal. There were five men waiting and Fic left me there telling the barber he would call back later. The barber had just finished cutting a man's hair when suddenly four German policemen barged in and ordered everybody out. This was the usual thing when they wanted a haircut. The five men hurried out and I just sat there. One policeman walked up to me and was going to swipe me across the face, when the barber said, 'He's deaf and dumb!'

'*Ach stumm!*' he said with a laugh, which reminded me of the laughing policeman. He picked me up bodily, told his colleague to get out of the chair, and sat me in it. The barber cut my hair, while they all sat round laughing. They thought it was a huge joke and I thought so too, when I offered money to the barber, the policeman brushed me aside and he paid. If only they'd known that the deaf and dumb Pole they were laughing at was an escaped POW.

Both Mietek and Max arrived the following Sunday. Max had heard of the episode in the barber's shop, but he wanted to hear it firsthand. 'Why didn't you go out when the others did?' he asked.

I told him things happened so fast. I found me just sitting there and the others had all gone, so I decided to play it out.

'Weren't you scared?' he asked.

'I was so scared that I put my hands between my knees to stop them from knocking.'

We had some more news to tell Mietek and Max. When we returned home from the incident at the barbers, little Feliks dashed out to tell us the Germans had brought the gelding back. They said it was gun shy. We hurried to the stable and when Fic saw the horse, he broke down and cried. The coat that used to shine like velvet was matted and cut with wheals. It was trembling with fright. When Fic spoke to it, I saw the old glint in his eye as he tossed his head; they'd not broken his spirit.

Before Max left, he caught my eye and I followed him out. Under the pretence of looking at the gelding he whispered, 'Don't tell anyone this, but I was talking to an officer on sick leave from the front. The Germans are gambling all on taking the Crimea and Stalingrad. If they don't succeed in a matter of weeks, they are going to have to retreat.'

That news bucked me up no end. It made a change for them to retreat and it would dent little Hitler's pride. It was just a year since the Germans had gone into Russia and such a lot had happened since then. I'd served my apprenticeship on the farm doing every job there was. Fic had lost his beloved horse and had it returned. Irena had persuaded her father to live outside the law, and now Kaszmira's prayers had been answered.

When I first saw the young man, he had one hand leaning on his bicycle and the other leaning on Kaszmira's shoulder, as he limped up the drive.

It was amusing how they'd met. He was riding through the village when he passed Kaszmira. She was so lovely, he couldn't resist turning his head. His front wheel went into a rut and that's how he fell for her.

I sat in the corner of the room studying him, as she knelt down in front of him, repairing the tear in the knee of his trousers because he was too bashful to remove them. He was tall, smart and good-looking with blond hair and yet I felt there was something about him that wasn't right. When she'd finished, he stood up and then I realised what was bothering me. He should have been wearing a square helmet and jackboots.

After that first meeting, he became a regular visitor. Sometimes he stayed all day and helped with the work. His father, who he didn't get on with, owned a big farm just outside Kalisz. I began to get worried, perhaps one of these days Kaszmira might whisper sweet nothings in his ear and forget what she was saying. I'd hate him to know who I was.

It was Sunday evening; I'd been down to the meadow with the horses and cattle all day. Baszka had fetched the cows in for milking and I was letting the horses graze a little longer. Kaszmira had been to see her boyfriend off and had taken a short cut across the meadows. She went to the horses and beckoned to me.

As I went over to her she said, 'Give me a leg up Stefan.'

'You've never needed a leg up before,' I said as I lifted her onto the mare.

'What do you think of my young man? Isn't he handsome?'

'Yes, he's certainly handsome and you've fallen for him, but I hope you never talk about me to him.'

She tossed her chestnut head just like the gelding as she replied, 'It wouldn't matter if I did, I can trust him,' and with that she rode off.

Mietek said goodnight to Gene, when I went into the farmyard and I beckoned him to come to the stable. I told him of my suspicions about Kaszmira's boyfriend and he said he would ask Max to try to check up on him.

While we were all working in the fields next day, Feliks arrived and said Max wanted Irena to go back to the farmhouse. When she returned everyone was curious to know what he wanted.

'He only wanted Sally's address. Someone wants to write to her,' she said. Later she asked me, 'Do you know what's going on Stefan because Max actually wanted to know if Kaszmira had a photograph of her young man? I found one in her handbag and he asked me not to tell her that I'd given it to him.'

I told her briefly of my suspicions.

I was looking forward to Sunday, Mietek would be coming to see Gene and perhaps he would have some news. It was a surprise to see Max and Mietek on Saturday evening. The look on their faces made me fear the worst. They had a few words with Fic and the three of them went into the other room. Fic asked Kaszmira and me to join them.

Max lost no time; he was really tensed up as he spoke. 'Kaszmira, I'm going to ask you a question, it doesn't matter whether the answer is "yes" or "no", but I must have the truth.'

The poor girl's face was deathly white; she was wondering what it was all about. 'Have you told your boyfriend anything about Stefan?'

'Yes!' My heart missed a beat, until she added, 'I told him Stefan was my cousin and his parents had been taken for forced labour in Germany.'

'Do you swear to that?' Max asked.

'Do you think I'm a liar?' Kaszmira demanded, 'and what business is it of yours?'

Fic answered her, 'You can go, I'll explain later.'

There was a look of relief on all three faces and I asked if my suspicions were correct. Max told me the young man was German. He had received his call-up papers and was trying to dodge them.

Mietek brought a bit of humour in the room by saying, 'He was trying to find a berth with the Fic family. It would have been interesting to have a German and an English POW under one roof.'

Fic told Kaszmira quietly that her boyfriend was a German. He never came to the farm again, as the authorities caught up with him. I expect Max was responsible for that.

In July, between the hay and corn harvest, most of the work was the dull monotonous job of hoeing. We were working in a field near the farm of the German called Shultz. He was working in the adjacent field with his wife and young son. He approached and started talking first in Russian and then in German, but none of us could understand him and so he left us and went to the farm to find Fic. They both returned and a real argument was going on. He counted us, then pointed to his wife, son and himself and counted three. A lot of Russian words are similar to Polish and I gathered he wanted Gene to work for him because she looked the most robust of the group. Gene told him to 'kiss her arse', but in Polish, it didn't sound so vulgar.

Next day he visited the farm waving a piece of paper. It was a work permit, signed by the district overseer for Gene to start working for Shultz the following day. Gene's first thoughts were to leave, but Fic reasoned with her. If she left, then Shultz would take one of the other girls. In addition, if she worked for Shultz she would be safe from the *lapanka*.

That night Gene came into the corn store where I slept and rummaged for the box of knives that had belonged to her grandfather. I looked at her as she slipped one of them in her blouse. 'If he tries anything with me Stefan, I'll kill him,' she said, and I'm sure she meant it.

The next day she was working in the adjoining field to me; there was no hedge dividing the field just a ditch. When she was close by, she called Irena over and told her the Germans were very excited over some news, apparently something important had happened.

I could hardly wait to go and see Wojciech. I wondered if he was still listening to the forbidden radio. Wojciech seemed just as pleased with the news as the Germans. Apparently they had taken Sevastopol and the Crimean oil fields. I asked him why he was so pleased.

'I don't believe they have taken Stalingrad, they haven't the strength. However, if they don't take it by autumn the Russians will come back at them when the weather changes. It's possible we could see them here in the spring.'

I only stayed one night and I was on my way back the next morning as Jan, Fic's nephew, wanted some help felling a tree. This was another undercover job as it was against the law. The tree had to be felled, sawn up, the roots dug up and no traces left.

It was about noon when I reached Modlibogowice. Passing the village store, I noticed two SS men having a drink outside. I'd walked about twenty yards when a voice shouted, *halt*.

This situation had gone through my mind a thousand times. I'd often pondered over what I'd do. I carried on walking and again came the call to halt. I had to check myself; I felt like running, the thoughts seemed to fly through my mind. Perhaps they would miss, but not at that range. Where would they hit me? Would they fire now or would they call again? I don't know if they called *halt* again, I just heard a woman screaming, 'Don't shoot! He's deaf and dumb!'

The woman from the store ran to take me back. I tried to act as if nothing had happened, but my legs felt like jelly. When they asked for my name and where I lived, I just stared vacantly. The woman from the store answered for me. They motioned for me to go, and a few minutes later, they overtook me on horseback. The one nearest to me flipped my cap over my eyes with his riding stick.

As they turned up the drive, I wondered how Fic would cope with them. When I arrived, they were laughing and joking, I know I didn't feel like laughing. I went to lie on the bed, I felt sick with shock. Later, when Fic called at the store, the woman said the German had put his rifle to his shoulder and was about to fire when she ran in front of him shouting who I was.

The next morning I didn't feel like going to Jan's to help him fell the tree. I was still feeling the effects of my narrow escape and my dreams had been full of it. It was a relief when Irena suggested going with me. Apart from the company, it was nice to have someone to explain if stopped.

I'd seen a tree felled many times before the war, but Jan's way was different, he wanted the root out as well, so we had to dig down sometimes as deep as six feet to chop through the roots. It was hard work, but fortunately, it was in the shade of the forest. It was late afternoon before there was any sign of the tree falling. Jan certainly knew his job and the tree fell just how he had planned.

It became obvious we weren't going to finish before nightfall and I could see Irena wasn't very happy about it. At the first opportunity, I asked what was wrong. She told me she didn't like staying over because Jan would want to take me to visit his friends. She explained that when Polish vodka wasn't available, they drank anything, methylated spirits or a homemade concoction.

'I don't have to go with him.' I reassured her.

'That would be worse. He would invite them here and I don't want to be around when they are drinking that stuff. Just try to be careful what you drink.'

Sure enough after supper, Jan put his coat on and pointed for me to do the same; frankly, I'd rather have gone to bed. As we went, I tried to note different landmarks, as I knew I'd be bringing him home drunk.

There were three men at the cottage when we arrived. The man who greeted us, I had not seen before, but I had met the others. Jan put his contribution to the party on the table, and the wife of our host hurriedly took it to the kitchen. She returned later with a large dish, which she placed in the centre of the table. Everyone ate out of the same dish. A party in Poland wasn't a family affair. The men sat round the table, the rest of the family huddled in the corners of the room. Our host went out and returned with four bottles. He was full of apologies for having no vodka, but he said his own special brew was just as good. Thank heavens when one of the bottles was almost empty, even so, there was still enough to make them all paralytic. One bottle contained methylated spirit and fruit juice. I never knew what was in the others, but they knocked it straight back and caught their breath. I had a glass of the methylated spirits and made sure I kept my hand over the glass after that, for our host was so anxious to top them up. At first they all seemed intent on getting me drunk, but as they had more to drink themselves, I was forgotten.

I was able to take stock of the rest of the family. In one corner was a little boy of about nine years old. He was playing with a pack of cards, but his interest seemed more on the conversation round the table. A girl, slightly older, was doing some French knitting. The woollen cord protruding out of the end of the bobbin looked as though it had been through the process a thousand times; I suppose it was her only plaything. A girl of about fifteen sat near her mother, she was supposed to be reading, but since the only light was a small oil lamp on the table, I think she was only going through the motions. Both mother and daughter had a worried, apprehensive look on their faces. I looked at their father and his only concern was to keep the glasses topped up. I thought if this was my family, I'd be worried the drinking would get out of hand. The girl looked up and gave a shy smile as she caught my glance. I had a feeling she was pleased one of us was staying sober. It was like waiting for a candle to burn out, waiting for those four men to flop or finish those bottles. By the time that the bottles were empty, two of the men were sprawled across the table and our host and Jan were sagging on their chairs.

What came next was so comical, just like a fire drill. The mother and daughter got hold of one man by the arms and feet, the younger daughter opened the door and they carried him to the barn. They returned from taking the second man and I'd just lifted Jan onto his feet, when he sprawled onto the floor. He too was despatched to the barn. Then the wife shook her husband, who was slumped on a stool, with his head on the table. There was no response, so she pulled the stool from under him and he fell back with a thud; he was a massive man. She touched my shoulder and pointed to his feet, she and her daughter held his arms. Once or twice, I had to smile as I felt them bump him on the ground as we carried him to the barn.

As I put on my cap and coat the woman said I could stay the night. When I took no notice, she pointed to the bed in the other room. I just waved goodbye and left. I felt sure I could find my way back to Jan's farm, but when I reached where the forest thickened, I knew I'd lost my way.

My mind went back to the day when I was a child and I visited the cottage in Oxcroft Wood. I again imagined my mother sewing the mangled body of Mr Ward in a sheet. That prompted me to run through the trees as though the Devil was after me. Eventually, I found the felled tree and from there I knew my way.

Next morning Jan's wife and Irena were anxious to know the whereabouts of Jan. It was easy, in sign language to tell them he was drunk. When he eventually arrived home, his hair and shirt collar were wet from having dunked his head in a bucket of water. Hangover or not, he knew he had to get that tree home before the Germans saw it.

His methods may have been crude, but they were effective and he soon had two pairs of wheels under that tree. Making sure there were no traces left, he fastened the horses to the wheels and off we went.

Once we arrived back at Jan's farm, Irena wanted to leave immediately, but he pleaded with her to stop and help saw it up. Once sawn up, it wasn't as noticeable as a tree trunk lying on the ground. Sawing a tree with a crosscut saw is like breaking a boulder with a toffee hammer. To give Jan his due, in between putting wet dock leaves on his head, he did his whack.

It was late afternoon when Irena and I started on the walk back home. We didn't mind this, as the evening was much cooler. As soon as we were at a safe place to talk, Irena wanted to know about the previous night. I told her all about how I'd sat there with one drink and watched the others get drunk, and how the mother and her daughter seemed frightened.

'Would that happen in England, Stefan?' she asked.

'I suppose it might a few years ago, but not in my home, I'm more inclined to worship my wife.' I wanted to say, 'put her on a pedestal', but I didn't know the Polish words.

Irena sighed, 'Yours must be a wonderful country Stefan and I shall never see it. Promise me, you will come back to see us after the war and bring your wife with you.' She looked at me, waiting for an answer.

'If I live, I'll come back, I promise. If my wife will come, I'll bring her too.'

The war news was so contradictory, so I decided to have a trip to Dziedzice to see if Wojciech had any definite news. I set off early after feeding the horses; Irena had risen to give me some breakfast. I hardly met a soul on the way, and as I passed the police headquarters at Trabczyn, I breathed a sigh of relief. Somehow, I never felt happy passing there, but it was a long detour to bypass it.

As I neared Zagorow, a huge closed-in lorry pulling two trailers drove towards me from the direction of Zagorow. As it passed, I noticed that the two trailers were also closed in, but the strangest thing of all, there was no smoke coming from the exhaust of the lorry or the first trailer, it was coming through a pipe on the last trailer. From time to time, I'd heard of the persecution of the Jews by the Germans. Wojciech Rewers told me how they were marched to the state farm near Dziedzice to work, and forced to sing a song about themselves, and they had a beating if they didn't. One day they all disappeared.

I should have turned right before I reached Zagorow and taken the short cut across the meadows. For some unknown reason I carried on towards Zagorow, my mind was still on that lorry and trailers. I wondered if they were full of Jewish prisoners. I didn't have to go through the centre of the town, but passing through the outskirts sent a chill down my spine, I felt I was walking through a ghost town. Apart from a few dogs, there was no sign of life. I saw no one until I reached Lad, two kilometres further on. A policeman stood on the bridge over the River Warta. I touched my cap and walked on, he just nodded. He looked as if he'd been there all night. As I walked through the village, a few people approached me and asked what was going on in Zogorow; I just carried on as if I'd not heard them.

When I reached Rewers' farm, Wojciech had heard that some people in Zogorow had been taken for forced labour. I told him of the lorry and how Zogorow was deserted and his face went white. He picked up his hat and coat and went out. It was afternoon before Wojciech returned with his face set.

'Well?' said Mrs Rewers.

'They arrived in the middle of the night with dozens of trucks and trailers; very few managed to get away.'

Later that night when we were talking he said, 'Stefan, it's diabolical. In a few weeks' time we shall be forced to buy patent manure made from their bodies. Those weren't just trucks, they were mobile gas chambers.'

He looked so full up, I couldn't ask him about the war news, but just before we were going to bed, I asked if he'd heard anything.

'Yes, I've listened to the radio every day for a week. They have taken Stalingrad and they seem to be still taking it. That's to boost morale. The truth is they can't take it, and they expect a big counter-attack from the Russians.'

'Will that be the end of it, do you think?'

'No! It's far from finished yet. They may pull back to the River Bug or even the Vistula,' he replied.

I returned to Modlibogowice the next day, saddened by the episode of Zagorow, but cheered by Wojciech's prediction: the Russians could be on the River Vistula soon and I'd be able to make it there.

This year when the corn harvest time came round, I felt more fitted to the task. In addition, people were more used to me; I was just *Stefan Nie Mowe*. The two German farmers didn't join in the pool to share labour and I was pleased. I didn't fancy going to cut their corn. Halfway through the harvest, the whole village had a surprise when they received a notice to report to the German farms. To add insult to injury it also said: *Bring your own food*. We had one day at each farm and then the begrudged task was over and we were able to carry on with an enjoyable harvest.

Just after the harvest, Shultz told Fic he wanted me to go and work for him. Fic tried to put him off by saying I wasn't very reliable. I was concerned because I thought he might go to the authorities as he had over Gene. I suggested to Fic that he could suggest I work for Shultz for a trial period. In addition, I suggested that he hinted that I was a bit unstable and had been known to go berserk. The German said if I went berserk with him, I'd get some whip.

My trial period lasted ten days; I couldn't stand it any longer. Shultz thought because I couldn't talk, I should be able to work like a horse. Even during the dinner hour, he would bring me extra tasks.

One particular day, I'd barely swallowed my dinner when he beckoned me to follow him. He took me to a pile of wood and pointed to a large axe on the chopping block for me to start work chopping wood. The sun was blazing hot; I could see Shultz and his family resting in the shade of a large tree. When it was time to return to work in the fields, he beckoned me to go. This was my chance. I jumped up as if a Zulu warrior, swung the axe round my head, and chased him across the yard. He made for the stable, which was the nearest building. I made sure I didn't catch him before he went in and slammed the door. I hit the door with the axe, left it there and went back to Fic's farm.

In the evening, Gene came to tell her father that Shultz wanted to see him. I asked her if my act had made any impression. She laughed as she told us how

Shultz was afraid to come out of the stable and he kept shouting until someone went to him. When he did come out, he had to go and lie down all afternoon.

I was anxious to know the verdict when Fic returned. Fic laughed as he told me what Shultz said, 'Fic, you should have him put away, he's too dangerous to be at large.'

'What did you tell him?' I asked.

'I told him he brought it on himself by making you work in the midday sun. Also I know when you are about to have a spasm and I lock you up.'

'Does he want me back?'

'No, I don't think so. He said you haven't to go near his farm again, or he will call the police.'

It was such a relief to get out of that situation.

By the autumn of 1942, the potato harvest was over, the peat dug and this time Kaszmira had been on her best behaviour. On the second anniversary of our escape, my thoughts were of Alex and Bomber. I wondered if they'd made it to Russia. Christmas came, and as Rewers put it, there was 'No present from Stalin.' The Germans were being hard-pressed, but still no concrete news. During January, we heard of the first Russian success. The Germans were retreating from the Caucasus. There was a spate of *lapanka* during the next few months; the Germans were trying to replace those called up for active service.

About the end of March, we were taken unaware, but Irena managed to get clear, thanks to the trapdoor from the cowshed up into the loft. Kaszmira wasn't so lucky.

She'd gone to the village shop and Baszka went to warn her telling her to make a detour across the fields. When we thought they'd gone, Kaszmira ran down the edge of the field joining the meadow and at that moment, a German on horseback suddenly appeared, galloping across the meadow. At the same time, Kaszmira disappeared. I shivered to think what she'd done; it took a lot of courage to jump in a ditch of freezing water. She would be up to her shoulders in water, that's if she kept her feet.

As soon as the German had gone, I raced down the meadow. She was blue in the face. I reached down, there was no time for ceremony and I grabbed that mop of golden red hair and dragged her up the steep bank. She screamed as I put her across my shoulder and hurried across the meadow.

Irena had some sand warming on top of the stove, and in no time, Kaszmira was in bed with hot sand bags round her. She nearly choked as Irena tried to force some vodka down her throat. A little colour came back into her cheeks; she had looked deathly white when Irena washed the mud off her face.

The following morning she seemed much better. I thought maybe she had just suffered from shock but our hopes were dashed later in the day when she developed a high temperature. She had a very high colour, the sweat stood on her brow and her lips were parched. I felt sure she had pneumonia and we took turns sitting by her bedside. During the night, she seemed to go into a coma, at times talking incoherently. It was two o'clock when Gene came to sit with her and I went to bed. The horses had a late feed the next morning because it was seven o'clock when I awoke.

There was an old woman from the village in the kitchen, bent over the stove, where two pans were boiling. I didn't know what was in them, but I could smell linseed. For three days, she hardly left Kaszmira's bedside. We were able to carry on working and whenever we looked in the room, she would shake her head as if to say 'No change'. On the fourth day, I looked in the room. The old woman beckoned me to the bedside, at first I thought Kaszmira was dead and the tears came to my eyes. 'She's over the worst now,' the old woman said, and realising I couldn't hear, she nodded and smiled.

While Kaszmira was ill, Gene worked for Shultz, and Irena and I had the brunt of the work. Loading manure out of the cowshed that had accumulated in six months, my arms seemed to be made of lead.

Fic had never joined in this work before and he seemed reluctant now, until Irena asked, 'When can we expect your highness to start using a muck fork?'

I didn't see much of Kaszmira because of being so busy. One day I went into the house and she was sitting by the window sewing. 'Did you think I was stupid jumping in the ditch?' she asked.

'You were brave; I don't think I'd have risked jumping in that water. What annoys me, is the callous way they hunt people and cause them to do what you did.'

Towards the end of May, I had to take an unplanned holiday. Mietek warned me the Germans were having a mobile chest X-ray unit in the district. According to them, Poles were riddled with tuberculosis and they wanted to keep a check. Max and Mietek advised me to go to Rewers for a few days while it was over. They thought a doctor would be able to tell if I was really deaf and dumb. It was their risk as well as mine, so I went to Dziedzice.

I stayed two days with Rewers. He had heard the pleasing news that the Germans had retreated out of Africa, and the Russians were advancing slowly, but too slowly to make me happy. Wojciech had said the Russians might soon be on the River Vistula. A thought popped into my head. This was an opportunity to travel about a little and see if I could still beg for my bed and breakfast. For seven days, I walked from place to place, begging my food, sometimes a bed, another time a barn.

When I returned to the Fic family in Modlibogowice, I'd been away for ten days, and they had all begun to fear the worst. In fact, Irena was on the point of visiting Rewers to find out what had happened to me. Fic informed me Max had fixed it that I been X-rayed and I probably had a dead man's chest on my records.

Max had some more news for me. Wojciech's words had come true, all the Polish farmers had to take a quota of that horrible patent manure, made from human bodies. True or not, I don't know, but the smell was different from any of the other fertilisers, it lingered in both the nose and the memory.

There were also some nasty rumours going round. The Russians had murdered many thousands of Polish officers. Max and Mietek were worried because their brother was an officer and taken prisoner. They hadn't heard from him since his capture.

The 22nd June arrived and another year had gone by. Could this be the last, I wondered? Another harvest and I began to feel depressed, so I went to Dziedzice.

Rewers was over the moon with the news, Mussolini had gone, Sicily taken, the British were in Italy and the Russians were slowly advancing.

A week later Irena walked down to the village and two police officers on a motorcycle and sidecar pulled up behind her. She was bundled into the sidecar and taken to the next village, where a lorry waited and from there to Germany. Mietek managed to see her before she left and she gave him a note for me. It said: *As I've looked after you, now you look after my family.*

Two anxious weeks went by before we heard from her. Was she on a farm somewhere or working in Germany? When we did hear, it was bad news, she was in a factory near Cologne; the censor had blanked out the name of the factory and what they were making.

Russian partisans had been active in the forest for quite a while, but now they seemed more adventurous. One night they paid a visit to Shultz's farm. After killing one of his pigs, they forced his wife to cook them a meal. They parcelled up the rest of the meat and left taking one of Shultz's horses with them.

The German police were very nervous as they patrolled the paths through the forest; you never saw just one police officer, mostly three or four together.

Once when Jan fetched me to give him a hand for a few days, we were stopped three times on the way. I was beginning to think it was safer to travel at night when the police kept a low profile, so the next time I had to make the journey to get some flour I travelled at night.

It was midnight when I set out for Jan's house and I seemed to set a chain of dogs barking as I passed each farm. It was a pleasure to reach the stillness of the forest where the creak of harness and the chink of a stone on the horse's hoofs were the only sounds on that October night. After a while, I'd have welcomed the bark of a dog, it was so eerie, with the moon casting moving shadows through the trees. With about three miles to go, there was a good stretch of road and I urged the horses into a gallop. The horses stopped suddenly and I nearly tipped out of the wagon. They backed away as if there was something on the road. I couldn't see anything, so I urged them on, but the gelding reared on his hind legs. I gave him a crack with the whip, which was something he wasn't used to. He plunged forward leaving me hanging onto the reins to prevent me going backwards. Something hit my shoulder and sent me sprawling across the seat and I struggled to bring the horses to a halt. I tied the reins to the wagon wheel and walked back to see what had hit me and frightened the horses. A man was hanging from a tree bough, swinging to and fro like a pendulum. I stopped in my tracks as I saw he was wearing jackboots. This was no place for me; I ran back to the wagon and rode out of the forest as quickly as I could.

What a performance trying to tell Jan what I'd seen, he wasn't very good at sign language so early in the morning. When eventually he understood he said, 'This place will be swarming with police at day-break,' as if I could hear him. His prediction was true, dozens of them probing, searching, asking questions. 'Who are you? Where have you come from? Why have you come here?' Jan must have satisfied them for they soon took their leave.

When Jan returned from the mill at midday, I heard him tell his wife the forest was alive with police, so I returned to Fic's by a long route to avoid the forest.

A week later, I couldn't believe my eyes as I saw a small figure trudging up the drive with a bundle under her arm. I felt sure I shouted 'Irena', as I rushed to meet her; if I did, no one was near.

No, she hadn't escaped as we first thought, but the factory destroyed by a bomb, and since other work couldn't be found, the workers had a month's leave. What a hope of Irena going back to forced labour of her own free will.

It would soon be the third anniversary since we scaled the wire. I wondered what had happened to Alex and Bomber.

It was almost time for Irena to return to Germany but she wouldn't talk about it. I went to Rewers at Dziedzice for a few days and I told them about Irena. Mrs Rewers said, 'Tell her to come and stay with us, she mustn't go back.' She had taken to Irena the moment she knew nothing underhand had been going on between us. At the end of her leave, Irena bid everyone goodbye and caught the train at Konin, as if she was going back to Germany, but she got off at Slupca, the town near Rewers' farm.

A week later, the Germans inquired about her and searched the farm. This was a daily routine for a while, until they became tired.

When I visited the Rewers, I found Irena hard at work. She'd found a sack of wool that someone had given Wojciech; it was just straight off the sheep – that's the reason she found it, because of the smell. She had washed and combed the wool, Wojciech had repaired an old spinning wheel and she was hard at work. All the Rewers family were proud of the new woollen sweaters Irena knitted for them. She told me she'd been happy doing something to earn her keep.

Nothing could stop her from going back home to Modlibogowice for Christmas. She had my bed in the corn store and I slept in the house; she was the one at risk now. The Germans didn't have the spirit of Christmas; they visited every day. On Christmas Day, they were well satisfied: they didn't catch Irena, but they caught two nice young cockerels. At New Year, Irena went back to the Rewers. Would it end this year I wondered?

There were rumours that the Russians were making headway now that the snow had come. It was about the middle of January when we heard they'd crossed the River Vistula. I couldn't believe it, there would have been more activity from the Germans if that were true.

Taking stock of things around me there was little reason to be optimistic: Irena was in hiding, Gene was working for Shultz, the work on the farm had to go on but somehow, I felt more optimistic than ever, I felt this was going to be the final year. Why, I didn't know.

Franc Fic Loses His Farm

I heard the Russians had retaken Odessa, but I couldn't get to Rewers to confirm it because the hay harvest was due. The district commissioner paid a visit. He looked over the stock, the buildings and then went into the house where he examined all the contents. Fic's proud possession, a handloom, had a lot of admiration. When he'd gone, Fic looked relieved saying, 'I thought he was going to take the loom.'

'I think we'd better make preparations,' I said, 'he's going to take more than the loom, he's taking the farm.'

I'd seen the pattern work out many times before, but I couldn't convince Fic. I went to the hide-out in the barn and pulled the wooden stakes out, letting the straw fall down.

Kaszmira followed me and said, 'You have me worried now, by doing that. Do you really think they will come and take the farm?'

'I'm certain they will. If I were you, I'd sleep in the loft for the next few nights. Ask Baszka to sleep with you.'

After supper that night, we sat talking. I asked Fic to let me take what grain he had to Jan's farm. That would make sure of flour for the coming months. No way could I convince him, and he laughed when I showed him my few worldly possessions packed in a bag, ready for off. I heard the patter of feet going up the ladder into the loft, the trapdoor above my bed opened slightly and I heard Kaszmira's voice saying, 'Don't forget to wake us if they come.'

They didn't come that morning, although I was up before daylight; it was like waiting to be hanged. Fic was jubilant, 'All this fuss over nothing,' he said, 'you'll be looking out until Christmas.'

The second and third morning came and Kaszmira and Baszka started ribbing me, they said I was kidding them.

'Tell me that tomorrow when I wake you,' I countered. My vigil didn't last long the following morning. I stood on the gatepost to get a good view up the road, but the dogs told me they were coming before I saw them. I banged on the house door and dashed to the corn store. Two white faces were peering down from the trapdoor; there was no need to wake them. They dropped down onto my bed from the trapdoor above. We hurried out of the back gate and across the fields.

They asked the same question at the same time, 'What are we going to do?'

My answer was rather sharp; I was annoyed we'd not made any plans. 'If your father had listened, we would have made some arrangements, now the only place we can go is to Widow Kaczmarek's.'

The elderly lady looked startled when she answered the door and saw the three of us standing there so early in the morning. After the poor woman got over her wailing and wringing her hands, she made us a cup of tea. I told Baszka to go home and let her parents know where we were. There was no danger of the Germans taking Baszka for forced labour, as she was too young. She returned in the afternoon to tell us to go to a house in the village, owned by a woman called Mrs Matuszewska and her son Max.

Fic and his wife were arranging the furniture when we arrived. Mrs Fic was heartbroken; the Germans had only allowed them to have two beds, a table and two chairs and the cooking utensils.

It was a small farmstead but since Mrs Maruszewska's husband had died, Max, had let it go to ruin. The single storey house had one door in the centre, which led to a small entrance hall littered with buckets, brushes and bits of harness. There was a door facing, which opened outwards. This was to a small storeroom filled with junk. A door on either side led to the two main rooms, both identical, about fourteen feet square. In one, Mrs Matuszewska and her son cooked, lived and slept. The other was to be the home of the Fic family until the end of the war. I helped to erect the stove, which was a metal box on legs with a steel pipe that went through the wall and curved upwards to form a chimney.

Mrs Fic prepared our first dinner of potato cakes: grated potato mixed with flour, flattened out and cooked on the stove. After we had eaten, Max beckoned me, he wanted to show me round and it didn't take long. The yard was about thirty feet square. Facing the house was a building about the size of the house; one half was the barn and the other the stable. In one corner stood an emaciated horse, and alongside it, a cow. A small area was fenced off in a ramshackle way, to house a few fowls.

There was a lot of straw in the barn. I thought it was a pity Max hadn't put some of it on the thatched roof. Looking up I could see more blue sky than thatch. When I looked at Max, I thought of something Irena once said about him, 'He's built for work, but not conditioned to it.' He was only prepared to work as a last resort. As we left the barn, he pointed to a harness hanging near the door, tied together with bits of wire and string. His sign language was easy to understand, he wanted some repairs doing and he was so disappointed when I shook my head.

As I lay on my bed of straw in the barn that night, gazing at the stars, I made up my mind that once Fic had settled down, I'd move on.

I decided I had to go to Rewers to see if he could help the Fic family, as they had no food. I set off next day; at the same time, Kaszmira went in the other direction to stay with her cousin Jan and his family.

When I told Wojciech what had happened to Fic he wanted me to stay with him. His argument was sound, the war was nearing the end and it was foolish to take chances. Somehow, I couldn't make up my mind. I felt like taking a chance and making my way to where the Russians were advancing. After staying two days I left with his warning ringing in my ears, 'Don't be a fool Stefan, we've all risked so much, don't throw it away now.'

Mrs Rewers wrapped up a large piece of ham and gave me strict instructions to throw it away, if I looked like being stopped. I was very cautious going back to Modlibogowice; I didn't want to throw that parcel away.

While I was away, the German who had arrived in Modlibogowice at the same time as Shultz had offered Kaszmira a job, so at least she was safe from *lapanka*. Fic had also been to some neighbours and found me a few casual jobs so he was surprised when I told him I was thinking of moving on.

Mrs Fic was amazed when she opened the parcel from Mrs Rewers. She had put their month's bread-ration coupons in as well as the ham. I felt choked as I thought about what the Rewers family had done for me.

After a few days, I weighed up the situation. Since Fic lost his farm, it was beneath his dignity to work for neighbours, so he was content to visit and have a chat with them and find work for me. Like it or not, I seemed to be the breadwinner for the family. Whatever work I did was paid for in some sort of food or milk.

Gene put the idea into my head. Shultz had inherited a few sheep when he took over the farm, and they were ready for shearing. Gene said it would be interesting to watch Shultz the next day because he was going to have a go at shearing them, but he'd no idea what to do. Long after she'd gone, I thought about it. Perhaps I could do some shearing for him during the night. The dogs would bark, but Shultz wouldn't investigate after the episode with the partisans.

About two o'clock in the morning, armed with a pair of scissors, a poor substitute for shears, I went to Shultz's farm. I knew where the sheep were kept. The dogs barked when the door creaked open. Closing the door behind me, I waited until they stopped barking and the sheep had quietened down. It was a work of art, feeling for a handful of wool and snipping. Straddled across a sheep and doing very well, but then it spun round and knocked me off my feet. One of them started bleating and they all joined in. When I'd snipped a large pile of wool and one or two fingers as well, I decided to call it a night.

I daren't go back to my bed in the barn, so I lay on some straw near the horse until daybreak. It took a lot of hot water to get the smell of sheep dung out of my hair and nostrils and my clothes had to be washed, but I'd a big sack full of wool that would keep Mrs Fic busy washing, combing and spinning.

The next day Gene called in to tell us the partisans had been to Shultz's farm again and would you believe it, they'd chopped the fleece off his sheep. She couldn't stop laughing when her mother told her what I'd done.

The previous year's potatoes were almost gone and the new ones weren't ready. Potatoes were the mainstay of the diet in Poland. They were eaten three times a day and so when the day arrived that we had nothing to eat something had to be done.

Fic wasn't very enthusiastic when I suggested paying a visit to the field at our confiscated farm, where we'd planted potatoes that spring. He mentioned one or two farmers who may have had some, but I knew he was stalling.

I set off with a sack under my arm about midnight. I hadn't gone far when I heard the patter of feet behind me. Standing in the shadow of a gateway, I waited. At first I thought it was Mrs Fic with a shawl draped round her and then I realised it was young Baszka. She nearly jumped out of the shawl when I stepped out of the gateway and asked where she was going. When she'd recovered she said, 'I'm going with you. It's a tedious job scratching round the roots for potatoes.'

Starting in the middle of the field, we scratched the soil from round the roots, pulling any decent sized potatoes we found and then replacing the soil. It became a nightly expedition.

Later when the German harvested his potatoes, he was disappointed at the poor crop, especially in the middle of the field.

The potatoes meant that we wouldn't starve, but another problem remained and that was clothes. I lost count of the times I heard, 'If only the Germans hadn't taken that linen.'

The German *kommissar* had taken Fic's loom, but worse still, he'd taken the linen that had been woven during the previous winter. At that time of the year, Mrs Fic would have it pegged out on the grass and repeatedly douched it with water to bleach it in the sun. Now it was gone.

One day I heard Kaszmira telling her mother how she'd been with her boss to a nearby German farm. He had so much linen pegged out to bleach in the paddock. When she'd gone, I asked Baszka if she knew where this farm was and I asked if she would take me there. Of course, she wanted to know why I wanted to go. I told her, 'Since it's such a big farm, I might find some work there.'

She looked disbelievingly at me, but agreed to take me. We walked about a mile from the village up a cart track, when she pointed to a farm saying, 'That's it.'

We walked past the farm; it was quite a large one by Polish standards. What I liked about it most was the strips of white linen laid out on the green grass.

'It's too risky Stefan.' Baszka said.

'What's risky?' I asked.

She gave a knowing smile. 'Do you think I didn't know why you wanted to come?'

'You're right Baszka; it's too risky, let's go home.'

However, I noticed a cornfield ran close to where the linen was pegged out on the grass. It would be possible to keep hidden in the corn for about a quarter of a mile or more. It was risky and it was wrong, but it was also possible. In addition, was it wrong to steal from someone who had already stolen it? Baszka promised not to mention where we'd been, and that was the end of the matter.

By noon the next day, I was in the cornfield at a point where I could see the farmhouse. A man and four girls came in from the fields; a buxom woman appeared at the door and shouted them in for dinner. The blood was tingling in my veins as if I was about to rob a bank, instead of eight lengths of linen. With one eye on the farmhouse door, I pulled each length in turn, hoping the pegs would come out of the grass before the linen tore. I dived into the cornfield dragging it behind me. It felt like I was dragging a marquee. When I reached the end of the field, a wide ditch divided it from the next field. Looking back, I'd left a trail that was plain to follow; so I rolled four lengths into a rough bundle, hurried along the ditch and then carried it into the next cornfield; it was as much as I could carry at one time. Then I fetched the remainder. Each time I reached the edge of a field, I repeated this process, until it was open fields. This was as far as I dare go in daylight, so I placed the bundles where I could find them at night, noting the number of paces from the edge of the field.

When I returned home to Mrs Matuszewska's house, she was in her room doing a little gossiping, so this prevented any awkward questions. It had taken so much out of me, I was exhausted and I felt inclined to call it off, but later that night I was on my way back to that cornfield. This time I had a knife to cut the strings attached to the wooden pegs, to lighten the load. Laying each length out on top of each other and then rolling them up neatly was a difficult job in a cornfield at midnight. Then with my heavy load, I made my way home.

I couldn't take the linen in the house as the door was locked. I took it to the barn, but the straw in the barn was so scarce I had difficulty in hiding the linen. At the first opportunity next morning, I took it in the house and I'll never forget the different reactions.

Baszka flung her arms round my neck saying, 'Stefan you've done it!' Mrs Fic reached for her rosary and mumbled prayers for forgiveness and Frank Fic's drooping moustache seemed to curl up as he gasped, 'You'll get us all shot.'

That summer, the Fic family were as smart as any family in the village. Irena made the dresses when she returned home. I looked quite smart as well, with a white linen coat and a pair of trousers dyed black.

As Mrs Fic was starting to get over losing the farm and things seemed better, fate dealt her another cruel blow. Irena was fitting Gene for her linen dress, when she said, 'When I've made this I think I'd better make some little ones.'

I turned round to see Mrs Fic fall in a dead faint. I rushed to pick her up and remembered something my mother told me. I sat her on the bed and put her head down between her knees. After a few minutes, she gained consciousness. Mrs Fic's health was everyone's concern. The cause seemed to be forgotten until later that night. When Mietek arrived he had some explaining to do. They had decided pregnancy was the only way Gene could get away from Shultz's farm. They hadn't thought that Fic would lose his farm and reduced to poverty and for the past few months both of them had been dreading this day. It wasn't possible for them to get married. This was another penalty imposed by the Germans on the Poles. Marriages weren't allowed. Shultz insisted that Gene worked right up to the birth. Perhaps for the best, with four sleeping and living in one room, five when Irena was at home.

Mietek was over the moon when he brought the news; the Russians had reached Praga, just across the river from Warsaw. He had it all worked out, the Poles in Warsaw would stand up and fight and the Russians would come across and help.

It was about a month later when the uprising started in Warsaw. Our hopes went sky high. I dashed off to Rewers to get the English news. Wojciech was elated as he spent hours listening to the radio. Britain was going to help the Poles all they could and their planes were already on the way. The bulletin ended with: *Remember the Russians are just across the river.* And that is where they stayed, just across the river; but worse still, they refused our planes permission to land. Without outside help, it was hopeless. The Poles took to the sewers and carried on resisting, but it was impossible without food and ammunition. We heard of many being captured and put against the wall and shot. Later on came the German reprisals. Warsaw was systematically blown up from the ground, the churches being the main target.

While all this was going on there were rumours of a landing by Allied troops in France. The Germans denied it at first, then later admitted a Dieppe-type landing had been made, but had been repulsed.

With the harvest in full swing, I hadn't had time to go to Rewers for the news. I couldn't expect the farmers to give me work in the winter if I left them in the lurch at harvest time. Now the Russians seemed to be content to stay on the banks of the Vistula, I came to terms with the fact that I was there for another winter.

The barn where I slept was ideal in the summer with a worm's eye view of the stars, but I'd not survive a night in winter. I thought of the small storeroom between the two living rooms of the house. At present, it was full of junk. With Fic's help, I managed to persuade Max his junk would survive a winter in the barn better than I would. Trust Max to suggest I moved the junk. My next problem was a bed. My old one was in the corn store at Fic's farm, unless the German had chopped it up.

Fic agreed to go with me the following day and as we went into the farmyard the German was trying to roll part of a tree trunk towards the barn. He immediately enlisted our help. As we dragged it into the barn, I saw my bed in pieces, but not chopped up. The German was reluctant to part with it; he would rather me stop and work for him and sleep on the bed in the corn store. Fic told him of the incident with Shultz and that did the trick, reluctantly he let us have it.

The bed just fitted in the storeroom without an inch to spare; it was fortunate the door opened outwards. I had to go to bed and then pull the door closed after me.

Reunited

At the beginning of September 1944, I went to Rewers' farm. Mietek prompted me; his German boss had confided in him that the Germans were mounting a counter-offensive against the Allied troops who had landed in France.

As I approached the farm, the whole family turned out to greet me. I thought it unusual, but when I asked if there was anything wrong, the answer was no. As we entered the house, I saw a man with his back to me, slowly he turned his head, and I gasped. In spite of the silly grin on his face, there was no mistaking Alex. No one would have thought we were two Englishmen. Alex talked in German and me in Polish, until Alex snapped, 'Why don't we speak bloody English?'

The next two hours were the hardest ever for conversation. It was unbelievable when I realised I was thinking in Polish, instead of English. Gradually, I heard the whole story of what had happened to him and Bomber, after they had left Rewers' farm.

Luck seemed to be with them all the way. They met a Pole who could speak English, and he gave them some useful information. He told them if they reached the American Embassy in Warsaw (America wasn't at war at that time) that was the link with the underground route back home.

It was late afternoon, fifteen kilometres from Warsaw and Alex was all for pressing on, but Bomber sat down, his feet were killing him and he couldn't go any further. Reluctantly, Alex agreed to look for somewhere to stay. They stopped at a farmhouse and a woman answered the door. Alex asked, 'Polish?' and she answered, 'Yes, but I can speak German.' Alex thought their luck was in, and when he asked if she would put them up for the night, she agreed. After a good meal and being shown to a bed in the barn, it looked as if their worries were over. Refreshed, the next day they would soon travel the fifteen kilometres to Warsaw.

It was a strange twist of fate that the woman's son arrived home on leave unexpectedly. She had not mentioned, that although she was Polish, she'd become a German citizen. The son had been called up for service in the German army and his reaction when his mother told him there were two English POWs in the barn was to summon the assistance of another German. They fetched Alex and Bomber and marched them to the nearest police station, five kilometres away. Helped along with a few kicks, Alex could barely keep up with Bomber. He summed it up by saying, 'Bomber nearly ran five kilometres to the police station, but he couldn't walk fifteen to freedom.'

They were sent to a camp in Germany, where a medical officer who examined them noticed Alex had been circumcised and branded him a Jew. He was beaten and questioned about what had happened to me. He stuck to his story that we had parted on the first night of our escape. Over the years, Alex had harboured the idea of escaping, but it wasn't until August 1944 that the opportunity arrived.

Although a heavy smoker, he'd deprived himself to save cigarettes to buy civilian clothes from the Germans. He also polished his pronunciation of German, until it was perfect. The rules in the prison camp weren't as strict as they were in the early days of the war.

One day, Alex was able to stay in camp on the pretence of being ill, while the others went to work. He changed into some civilian clothes, and with a briefcase under his arm, he looked so important with his swinging walk, that the young German soldier on the gate never questioned him.

It was when he arrived in the town, he noticed people staring at him. At first, he couldn't think why. Then he suddenly realised, he seemed to be the only person carrying a briefcase, who wasn't wearing a hat. Alex, always a quick thinker, went into a bar and ordered a drink. Looking round he saw a hat stand with a number of hats. After drinking his beer, he walked casually to the rack and put one of the hats on his head. Making his way to the railway station, he asked for a second-class ticket to Slupca.

Slupca was the nearest station to where he'd left me in Dziedzice. The ticket clerk asked for his permit. Alex made an excuse; he'd left it at home. 'You are not allowed to travel more than fifty kilometres without a permit,' said the clerk.

'Can you book me as far as the fifty kilometre limit? I shall have to try to get a lift from there.' He wasn't lying when he added, 'It's essential that I get there today.'

Alex was feeling pleased at getting over that obstacle when another arrived, in the form of a ticket inspector. Alex was in a first-class carriage with a second-class ticket. Alex explained he'd boarded the train in a hurry and he was quite willing to pay the difference. The inspector made out the excess ticket and Alex gave him the money. Alex felt so pleased with himself, he pulled a packet of Players cigarettes out of his pocket and handed them round. A German officer took one and nodded to Alex saying, 'From British POWs?' That was Alex all over, sheer bravado.

He left the train and faced the prospect of waiting until the following day for a train, or walking the rest of the journey. He was surprised at the number of lifts he received on farm carts during daylight. Speaking in German, no one dare refuse him, but when darkness fell, he had to walk the rest of the way. A very weary Alex hobbled up to Rewers' farm in the early hours of the morning.

We had been talking for so long. Wojciech was feeling out of it, so I asked him about the war news. It was true; the Allies had landed and established a broad front. The Germans had counter-attacked but without success. Wojciech sounded so pessimistic I had to ask, 'How long do you think it will last?'

His answer was just as gloomy, 'For you it could be soon, for me, a long time, possibly never.'

'Why do you think that?' I asked.

'First it was Katyn and now Warsaw. The Russians don't intend for there to be a Polish state, unless it's under their supervision. We shall be betrayed Stefan,' he said sadly. He looked at the clock, which was a sure sign he didn't want to continue with that conversation. As I stood up to go, he said, 'There are more important things to talk about, but I'll talk to you tomorrow.'

Alex and I went to the barn to sleep, but somehow I felt restless.

'Is there anything wrong between you and Wojciech?' I asked.

'Nothing wrong really, he gets on my nerves a bit, he's so jumpy. He's scared of his own shadow.'

'What gives you that impression? Have the police been round?'

'No,' he said, 'I got bored being cooped here, so I decided to have a walk round and when I returned, he nearly went mad.'

'Did you have a row over that?'

Alex laughed, 'How can you have a row with someone when he can't speak your language and you can't speak his?'

I knew that tomorrow Wojciech would want me to tell Alex what he could and couldn't do.

Wojciech lost no time next morning. After breakfast, he beckoned me to follow him up to the loft and closed the trapdoor. He looked serious as he sat down on a heap of sacks and pointed for me to do likewise. He started to go round the issue saying, 'I've always done my best to help you Stefan and you've always played the game.'

'I thought you wanted to talk about Alex?' I said, interrupting him.

'I don't want to talk about him, I want you to get him away from here before he gets us all shot.'

I was in a flat spin; this was more serious than I thought. Get away to where? Things were bad enough at Fic's and they would be worse when Gene returned home to have her baby. Who could I trust? Who could I ask to take such a risk and shelter Alex? To gain time to think, I said, 'Tell me what Alex has been doing to cause you to feel like this.'

'Your friend is very brave,' he said, 'but, he's recklessly brave and that's no use in this situation.' He pointed to a door in the far wall; from there you could look down the drive and beyond as far as the village. 'He opened that door and was looking out when he'd been told to keep out of sight. Country people are inquisitive. If they see someone up there and they have not been introduced, they think you are hiding someone. Another time, he was looking over the fence when I was having a word with a neighbour who was passing. The last straw was the other day, he went out walking, he was away two hours and when he returned, he passed that same neighbour. He has no papers and he can't speak Polish, although he can speak German. I've been thinking, why not ask the nephew of Fic to have him? Then he could walk in the forest all day.' It seemed that Wojciech had made up his mind.

'That means letting someone else know our identity, doesn't it?'

'I regret that,' Wojciech said, 'but that's the lesser of two evils.'

When I left Rewers' farm next morning, I had a load on my mind. I told Wojciech I'd sort it out one way or another, and would be back in four days. It wasn't just a matter of asking Jan if he would shelter Alex, there was also Max and Mietek to consider – how would they react to letting someone else know?

The news came as a bombshell to the Fic family. They only knew Alex by my reference to him, but Max and Mietek both agreed that the best person to ask to shelter Alex was Jan; his farm was isolated and near the forest.

Our plans didn't materialise. When Jan got over the shock of knowing his deaf and dumb cousin was really an English soldier, we asked if he would be prepared to shelter my friend. He obviously looked for a favourable excuse. He said the Germans visited the farm regularly and he had his children to consider.

He suggested an alternative when he mentioned a party of Russian partisans who visited regularly. Why not join them? According to Jan, they visited varying their time from between five to ten days. They would do their washing, prepare food, rest and take things easy. They never arrived empty-handed, always with an abundant supply of meat. They were due to call any day, but Jan never knew just when. It was agreed, Jan would ask if Alex could join them. Rewers seemed pleased with the idea when I went back and told him. I agreed to fetch Alex as soon as the arrangements were finalised.

Rewers wasn't very happy when I told him I was going as well. He raised all kinds of objections until I told him that Alex and I had started out together and we would succeed or fail together.

Almost a week went by before Irena came with the news that Jan had made the arrangements and we were to go to his farm as soon as we could. I went to Dziedzice to collect Alex. Although I'd told them I was going with Alex, they never seemed to take it in. To them I was part of the family. It was when I started getting my belongings together that they started to realise I was really leaving. Mrs Fic was heartbroken. I was so upset too when she said, 'It seems you are the third son I've lost.'

Gene and Kaszmira both tried to persuade me not to go, but Irena was the worst. She called me all the fools she could think of and her parting shot was, 'We have tried to keep you safe for your wife and you throw it away for a friend.'

Jan was pleased to see us, although we had a two-day wait before the arranged meeting with the Russian partisans, when he would take us to the meeting place in the forest. When I asked why they didn't come to the farm, he said they never made a prearranged meeting at a house, always in the open.

Those two days of waiting were very uncomfortable. Jan's wife and children still thought I was deaf and dumb, but they were puzzled about Alex. Jan had not told them who he was.

The meeting place was where a path crossed a cart track in the forest, and the time arranged between eleven and midnight. We waited for what seemed hours and I guessed it was after one o'clock, when we heard the sound of rifle fire. A little later, again this time much nearer, more sounds of shooting. We moved to where we could see down the cart track, hidden from sight, and waited. Five or six men came down the track; at first, we thought they were the partisans, until we heard the sound of their voices. Alex whispered, they were moaning about having let someone get away, all I could understand were their curses. After another hour of fruitless waiting, we decided to go back to Jan's home.

Early next morning, Jan went out to see if he could get any news, while Alex and I hid in the forest, where we could keep watch. Jan discovered that the previous night, a German SS patrol saw a man in the forest and called on him to halt. The man didn't halt and then four or five men, from both sides of the path, fired at them. One German had a bullet wound in his arm. The man the Germans challenged was the advance guard for the group of partisans. Jan said he thought the partisans would move away for a time. I thought it was a broad hint for Alex and me to leave, so the following morning we went straight back to Rewers.

The war was in its final stages, we thought probably just a few more months. I decided to put it to Wojciech, if he couldn't shelter Alex for that length of time, we would both try to make it to the Russian lines.

The Rewers family were overjoyed to see us, especially Mrs Rewers. Somehow I never got round to asking them to shelter Alex because Wojciech said, 'We shall see this through together.'

I returned to Fic at Modlibogowice, and for me it was back to the old routine. There was so much work to do before the winter set in. As the autumn ended, I went back to Rewers as often as I could. Primarily to hear the news, but also to see how Alex was behaving. The Allies had established themselves in France and the German counter-attack had come to nothing. If only the Russians would move, but Wojciech didn't think they would until December or January. The Germans were digging lines of trenches to stem the Russian advance or rather the Poles were digging under German supervision.

Irena

A day to remember was the sixth of November, my thirty-first birthday. The dreaded *lapanka* seemed a thing of the past, when out of the blue they swept through the village. It was late afternoon. Irena crossed the yard to fetch some peat for the stove. One of the German police saw her as he passed, vaulted the gate and grabbed her. Without waiting for her to get a coat, they bundled her into the wagon. Mrs Fic was distraught; November in Poland could be terribly cold. She insisted that Fic went to Rychwal to see if he could find where Irena had been taken.

All we knew when he returned was that she'd been taken first to Konin and from there they'd left in a lorry. When Mietek came from work at the council offices that night he was able to tell us that Irena had gone to a camp just beyond the town of Kola on the main Poznan/Warsaw road. When Mrs Fic heard, she asked me to take Irena a parcel of warm clothing.

It was strange riding a bicycle. I hadn't ridden one for years and Fic's boneshaker had seen better days, but I felt so happy. I nearly started whistling 'Colonel Bogey'.

Kolo was roughly sixty kilometres away and the camp was about three kilometres beyond. When I arrived at the camp, I saw two long wooden huts and nearby a field kitchen with spiralling smoke. I thought of my POW days, with grains of meat and gallons of water. A tall wire fence, mostly rotted away, surrounded it. Two wooden gates gave entrance from the road; they were wide open, there didn't seem any point in closing them. Across the field, I could see a line of people digging trenches. I cycled back up the road to where I'd seen a haystack in a field and I hid the bicycle behind the stack. Returning to the camp, I hung around until the prisoners were marched back to camp. As the prisoners stood in line I walked up to the guard and pointed to the bundle under my arm and then to Irena who was standing in the line.

'What do you want?' snapped the German. I didn't answer, merely pointed again to the bundle and then to Irena. He grabbed my arm and took me to Irena, demanding, 'Who is he?'

Irena explained I was her cousin and deaf and dumb.

'*Ach stumm!*' he said, giving me a slap on the back.

Irena took me to the hut. Inside there were no beds, just rows of straw bales and no bedding. The shout came for everyone to line up for supper and the guard loaned me the lid off his mess tin to get some soup. As soon as we'd finished the soup I took the lid back to the German and pointed out I was leaving. He shook hands with me. When no one was listening, I asked Irena about the security. She told me they were counted into the hut at night and then the door was closed and not opened again until morning.

'What about the toilets?' I asked.

'There's a row of buckets at one end of the room. Imagine what it's like with all the windows barred,' she answered.

'I'm taking you home tonight,' I said.

'No, Stefan, it's too dangerous. If you get caught they will be suspicious about you.'

'If you stay here you will be eaten away with lice or die of fever. I'll see you later,' I said and walked away.

I'd noticed the Germans billeted in a mobile van, similar to the ones used to transport the Jews. I walked round the camp on the outside of the wire and stopped at a point nearest to the huts. Walking over the trampled, broken wire, I crept up to the hut. There was hardly a sound from inside. It wasn't much of a camp to break into, but it made a change from breaking out. A sound of laughter was coming from the van, a light was shining through the window and the huts were in darkness. There was no sign of a guard; with both huts locked from the outside, there didn't seem to be the need. As I walked round the hut, the door of the van opened and a German stepped out. The chink of light fell on the hut a few yards beyond where I stood. The German walked down the side of the van and stood, it was obvious they had a row of buckets for a toilet. The German returned to the van and closed the door.

The door of the hut was fastened by a piece of wood slotted through two brackets. Pulling the wooden bar across, I slipped into the hut and closed the door behind me. It was so dark; I stood for a few minutes to get my bearings. I felt a tug at my arm; Irena had seen me come through the door. We slipped out unseen and slid the wood fastener back into position. We made for the wire, keeping the hut in between the mobile van and us.

The cycle was still near the haystack where I'd left it. The bundle of clothes made a temporary seat on the crossbar and we were homeward bound. Perching on the bundle of clothes caused Irena's legs to get in the way of the steering and we had a few falls, until she decided to sit with her legs over the handlebars.

When we arrived home at two o'clock in the morning, Mrs Fic was still waiting up. She was overjoyed to see Irena. I could see her fingers going up and down her rosary; she thanked God for everything.

I woke Irena at eight o'clock, but she was reluctant to get up. I went outside for a moment, then ran in giving the signal we had for the German police. In two seconds, she was out of bed and through the back window. She was furious when she realised it was a false alarm. I reminded her it wouldn't be a false alarm later on and she should get on her way to Jan's because they would be looking for her.

They searched the farm for her later that morning, but she was well on her way by then. Mrs Fic told them she'd sent her clothes to the camp and as far as she knew, she was still there.

Gene left Shultz's farm and came home; her baby was due any day. The room where they lived and slept seemed to be bursting at the seams. I felt sorry for Mrs Fic; somehow, she just couldn't face up to it. She had not been outside the gate since the news leaked out about Gene. It was difficult to understand why two people were deprived of the right to marry and give a name to their child. Mietek called every morning before he went to work; he was so worried until he heard the elderly woman saying she'd delivered every baby in the village for the past thirty years. They fetched her in a panic one morning. She examined Gene and told them to stop worrying and she left saying, 'I'll be back at five.' Gene had a baby daughter at six o'clock that night. Everyone seemed disappointed; somehow, the Poles had a craving for boys.

Of all my time in Poland, this was the most aggravating. A feeling of stagnation, nothing was worth doing, everyone knew the Russians were coming; the question was, when? The sixth of December passed again; another year.

No one had inquired about Irena after that first search and so she returned home a few days before Christmas.

The Polish people made quite a lot of Christmas. A candle burned in the window of every house in the village. My thoughts were on the following week, New Year's Day. It was on everybody's lips: *Nowy Rok,* the day the Russians were coming.

I left for Rewers' farm and there was nothing on the news to indicate the Russians were about to advance. I wasn't disillusioned; you wouldn't expect them to advertise it. Wojciech showed little excitement. The German overseer, who had confiscated the pig that

Wojciech had planned to kill for Christmas, had ruined his Christmas.

I was awake before daybreak on New Year's Day, and as soon as Wojciech rose, I was pestering him to fetch the radio. This annoyed Mrs Rewers, who made no secret of the fact she hoped the Russians would never come, 'Better the Devil you know,' she said.

That evening I stood by the well looking down at my reflection in the water when Wojciech asked. 'Why are you so miserable Stefan?'

'Miserable,' I said, 'I feel like going down there head first.'

'Don't be so disillusioned,' he said, 'it isn't the Russian New Year until January 6th.'

It started snowing next morning, so I decided to go back to Modlibogowice to see Fic. They would be eager for news, but I could tell them nothing. The next two weeks seemed like two years. It was the evening of 12th January 1945, when Mietek arrived from Konin. His German boss had told him in confidence that the Russians would attack within the next forty-eight hours and if the German front line failed to hold them, they had to evacuate to Poznan.

I left for Rewers' farm next morning as I knew Alex would be anxious for news and I wanted an understanding of what Alex was going to do. I didn't fancy telling the first Russian officer to come along who we were, as I preferred to wait and see what their attitude was first. Two days later, we heard that the Russians had launched a three-pronged attack. When I said I was going back to Fic's, Wojciech was surprised. He pointed out there were more places to hide with him, if the occasion arose. I felt I had a duty to go back to Fic. He could need help, so after dinner I set off.

I'd only gone a short distance and I was approaching the crossroads where I should turn off for Lad. An elderly woman, wrapped in a large shawl, hobbled towards me. She was carrying what looked like a heavy parcel. As she drew level, she asked me in Polish, 'Am I on the right road for Ciazen?'

At first, I didn't answer, but looking round and seeing no one in sight, I decided to take a chance. She was an old woman with a large parcel, going in the wrong direction.

Speaking in Polish, I explained she'd taken the wrong turn at the crossroads. As she walked with me to the crossroads, I pointed out the way. As she left her parting words were, 'God bless you for being so kind.' Her prayer must have fell on deaf ears, for the next minute a German policeman jumped out of the ditch. Prodding his revolver in my stomach, he asked for my identity paper. There was no point in giving him that, which stated that I was deaf and dumb, after he'd heard me talking to the old woman. My only hope was to bluff it out.

I explained I'd been working in Germany and had come home on leave. He asked where I lived and I said Zagorow. Again, he asked for my identity paper and I said I'd left it in my other coat at home. He wasn't taking any chances; quite a few German policemen had come to grief when they challenged a partisan. With his revolver still pressed in my stomach, he tapped my pockets to see if I was armed. He then told me to turn round and with the revolver in my back, marched me down the road towards Ciazen.

I varied my stride to see if it would relieve the pressure of the revolver in my back, but it didn't. I wondered if the safety catch was on. Unless there was a chance to make a break for it before I reached the police station and the chances looked remote, I was going to have to do some explaining.

The identity paper in the top pocket of my coat was useless now and I realised I'd better get rid of it. Feigning a bout of coughing, I slipped the folded scrap of paper from my pocket into my mouth. Thank goodness the paper was thin and flimsy, but what a job I had rolling it round my mouth until I was able to swallow it without the policeman noticing.

Next, I had to think of an explanation. First and foremost, I had to move the scene away from that locality, for if they made inquiries, someone may have recognised me and connected me with Rewers. By the time we reached the police station in Ciazen, I'd worked it out.

The policeman pointed to a chair and told me to sit down. He removed the rifle from his shoulder and went to put it in a rack in the corner. What a pity he'd locked the door as we entered. Then he searched me thoroughly. He found nothing, so he sat down at the table and took up a pen and paper.

'What is your name?' he asked in Polish and then added, 'And don't tell me lies or you will be sorry for it!'

I didn't intend to tell lies. 'I'm Colin Marshall, a British soldier,' I said in English.

With a look of amazement on his face he said, 'Speak Polish. Tell me in Polish who you are.'

So I told him I was a POW who had escaped four years previously and had lived among the Polish people ever since. He asked where I'd lived and I told him Grodzisk, a small town southwest of Warsaw. My idea was to give him the impression I was just passing through when he'd stopped me. He asked why I'd left Grodzisk and I told him I didn't want to be a prisoner of the Russians.

'Where were you making for?'

'Anywhere west.'

'How long have you been in the locality and why were you on a byway and not the main road?'

I named a place about twenty miles away, where I said I'd spent the night. I told him I'd no map; I just kept on walking west. I'd been trying to beg food and drink, but the people seemed so mean in that locality, and I hadn't had anything since early morning. He rapped the table, a woman came to the door, and he let her in. He told her to bring me food and drink. I thought the interrogation had finished. He stood up and walked across the room.

Turning suddenly, he snapped, 'You are a stranger and you have no map. So how could you tell that old woman the way?' His tone was accusing; I had to think fast.

'The woman asked if she was on the right road for Ciazen and I knew I hadn't passed through that place, so I told her she was on the wrong road. When we reached the crossroads, I saw the sign post and pointed out the road.'

'Were you coming to Ciazen?' he asked.

'No I was going in the opposite direction, to the west.'

A woman brought a plate of bread and dripping and a mug of coffee. She fussed around, obviously wanting to say something to me, until the policeman shouted at her to go. When I'd finished eating, he led me to a door. He put a heavy chain round my wrists, fastened it with a lock, and then opened the door to what looked like a coal store. The windowless room was about seven feet by four feet, with a pile of coal at the far end. I hesitated for a moment; the German policeman gave me a powerful shove and slammed the door. After standing for a while trying to get my bearings, I started to feel round the wall. If this was a coal store, it was possible there was a trapdoor from the outside wall. After going round the walls, I found there was only the door I'd entered, so any hope of escape had gone. I sat down on the heap of coal and after a while, I fell asleep; how long I slept, I don't know.

I dreamt of my life in Derbyshire: my mother, the pit, army life and my wife. I stirred uneasily as the coal dug in my back. Then I shot upright, this was no dream; it was real.

I saw a chink of light under the door and heard the sound of heavy objects being dragged downstairs. I hammered on the door with my fists and kept hammering until someone opened the door. The same policeman led me to the toilet and made me leave the door open. When I came out there was another German in the room; by the insignia round his collar, I gathered he was the boss. They were having a heated argument, and though my knowledge of German was limited, I knew I was the cause of the argument. The policeman argued, I'd evaded capture for so long and he'd captured me, so I should be taken with them.

There was little enthusiasm in the commandant's voice when he replied, 'Take him, shoot him or do what you please with him. I've a wife and two children to think about.'

That seemed to settle the argument. The policeman took a key from the table and unlocked the chain round my wrists. He went to the rack, picked up a rifle, and pointed to the door. He told me in Polish to go. He followed me to the door. A path led straight from the door to the road. As I walked down that path, I expected a bullet in my back at any moment. It seemed such a long path. Was he going to shoot me as I reached the road I wondered? The moment I turned onto the road, I ran as if the Devil was after me. It seemed incredible that they'd let me go.

After walking round for a while to make sure that I wasn't being followed, I made my way back to Rewers. What a welcome I received. The woman at the police station, who served me food and drink, had told people in the village that an Englishman had been arrested, and they knew it must be me. Wojciech hugged me saying, 'I never thought I'd see you alive again.'

We heard the next day that the Russians had started their advance and the Germans were moving out. I would have returned to Modlibogowice that afternoon, but I could see Wojciech had something on his mind. During the afternoon, I asked what it was.

'I'm trying to look into the minds of the German Command. Somewhere they will have to make a stand and it is feasible they could counter-attack along the Vistula from the south and we would be back to square one.'

I knew what was bothering him; he had it in his mind to fetch the pig back that the German had taken at Christmas, but he was worried. I had a word with Alex and we decided we would do it. The German didn't know us from Adam, so if he saw us it wouldn't matter.

Soon after dark, in spite of Wojciech's objections, we took the horse and sledge and went to the German farm. Tethering the horse outside, we made our way through the farmyard. The house was in darkness, but a movement of the curtain told us the farmer was still there. All the Germans had service rifles, so there was a chance he may have taken a shot at us, but there was no sign of life until we opened the door of the pigsty. I went inside and closed the door before lighting the lantern we'd brought. Alex stood outside to keep watch. There was no telling which one belonged to Wojciech, so I went into the pen of the biggest pig. The plan was to stun it, truss it up and hurry back to Rewers, but once I'd stunned it, I had to put it out of its misery. With the pig trussed up and slung from a pole across our shoulders, we hurried across the farmyard to the waiting sledge.

Leaving the pole behind, we drove off as fast as the poor old horse could go. Really, there was no need to hurry; the whole village was in darkness, people waiting behind locked doors, most in apprehension as to what the Russians would bring.

As we went through the gate to Rewers' farm, a thought crossed my mind: this was the first time I'd brought anything; I'd always taken something away.

I wanted to be up early next morning, to be in Modlibogowice before the Russians came. It was just breaking daylight when Mroz's bark woke us. A woman came to the farm. She brought news: the Germans who had taken Piotr Rewers' farm all those years before had left during the night, so Mrs Rewers and I had to go there to milk and feed the stock.

It was eleven o'clock by the time I was ready to leave for Modlibogowice and the family came to the gate to see me off. We saw a figure in a grey German uniform coming up the road to the farm, but when he saw us, he cut across the fields and made towards two small farms about half a mile away.

There was a frightened note in Mrs Rewers' voice when she said, 'The woman in the second farm is on her own.'

Alex and I dashed across the fields and we saw the German going to the second farm. We were a good distance away when we saw him enter. A man, possibly the farmer, dashed out of the other farm and went after the German. They came out of the door together, locked in a struggle. The German had a revolver in his hand. The farmer gripped his wrist and forced it back; the gun fell to the ground. The German broke away and as he did so, he pulled a grenade out of the top of his jackboot and threw it through the farmhouse door. The explosion blew the windows out. When the smoke began to settle we were able to see what had happened.

There were bits of metal all over the place. The grenade had landed either on or under the stove and blown it to bits. A woman was moaning in the corner, a small pool of blood dripped from a wound, but she started struggling like mad when we tried to see where. A piece of metal had gone through her clothing and lodged in her thigh near the groin. I looked around, there was nothing suitable for bandaging; so I took off my shirt and tore it up. That poor woman was suffering, but no way would she allow us to disturb her clothing to bandage her until Mrs Rewers arrived and persuaded her. We bandaged her as best we could, but she needed a doctor.

Wojciech had already gone for his horse and cart. I thought of the revolver the German had dropped. I thought the farmer would have picked it up, but I think the explosion had shaken him up too much. It had fallen behind a bucket. There wasn't much time to inspect it as Wojciech arrived with the transport. As I put it in my pocket, I noticed it was a Luger automatic.

The doctor was out when we arrived at his house in Ciazen, but his wife asked us to wait. She made the woman comfortable on a couch and gave her a cup of tea. It was late afternoon when the doctor attended to her. Wojciech had gone home on foot leaving Alex and me with the horse and cart. We gave the woman a chair lift down the garden path, her face was deathly white.

Two Russian soldiers walked through the gate towards us. One of them started questioning us in Russian, but I didn't understand what he was saying. This annoyed him and he pulled a revolver out of his belt and waved us back into the house. Fortunately, the doctor could speak a little Russian and after a short conversation with the Russian, told us to take the woman back into the surgery. He explained that he was also a doctor and he wanted to have a look at the woman's wound. Still waving the revolver, the Russian ushered us outside and slammed the door. What happened inside we didn't know. We waited quite a while then suddenly, the curtains at a nearby window parted. The woman opened the window and she threw herself out; head first. I picked her up from the ground and lifted her across my shoulder and we ran to the cart. We were away as the Russian ran down the path.

After Mrs Rewers had made the poor woman comfortable and revived her with a stiff glass of Wojciech's firewater, she told us what had happened.

The Russian ordered the doctor out of the room and motioned the other Russian to leave the room also. Then he lifted her onto the couch and removed the bandages. When she realised he was going to rape her, she started to struggle, but he was strong. She stopped struggling and went limp. The Russian dashed out for something to revive her. God gave her strength to get off the couch and push a chair under the door handle. Then she opened the window and in her own words, 'Fell out.' Sickened by the day's events, I went to bed determined to go back to Modlibogowice.

I left Rewers' farm early. I knew Wojciech didn't want me to go, but I felt I had a duty. I saw the first sign of the war when I reached Lad. The wooden bridge across the River Warte that I needed to cross had almost disappeared, the remains still smouldered.

Wojciech had some friends in Lad. They lived by the river and owned a small rowing boat. I remembered Wojciech once told me if ever I found the bridge guarded, his friend would take me across. Most of the cottages near the riverbank had names of the owners on a board outside. The man's name had slipped my memory; I just knew the name ended with 'bowski'. I arrived at a cottage with a sign *'Boleslaw Yakabowski'*, and a man was clearing the path outside. I asked him in Polish if he knew Wojciech Rewers.

'He is a friend of mine, but why do you ask?' he replied.

'Wojciech told me if I had trouble getting across the river, you would take me.'

'What's your name?' he asked suspiciously.

'Stefan Wysocki,' I said.

'Stefan is deaf and dumb', he replied and the tone of his voice told me I was going to find it difficult to convince him. It sounded stupid when he asked to see my identity paper and I told him I'd swallowed it when arrested by a German policeman. 'Why did you do that?'

I was getting nowhere, so I decided to tell him the truth. I told him I was an English soldier and a POW who Wojciech had befriended.

'How many brothers did Wojciech have? What were their names and their children's names?'

Finally, convinced, he invited me into his cottage. I explained I was in a hurry, but to no avail. He wasn't going to miss such an opportunity. He'd never met an Englishman before. When he suggested introducing me to his friends, I walked out of the house and down the path to the river. He quickly followed, full of apologies as he ferried me across the river. We shook hands and I thanked him and hurried on my way.

The police headquarters at Trabczyn were deserted; no sign of German or Russian soldiers alive or dead the whole journey.

Feliks ran to meet me, followed by the family. Everyone hugged me, including Kaszmira. As we walked up the drive, I began telling them what had happened. A neighbour stood by the gate; she was staring at me, her mouth wide open as if she was trying to say something. 'He can speak!' she gasped in amazement.

Mietek was worried about the fact I'd swallowed my identity paper. He was still working for the council in Konin at this time, but now supervised by the Russians. The Russians were checking everyone's papers and if anyone didn't have a Polish identity paper, they were taken into custody.

He brought a blank paper with just the German stamp on it and an ink-pad for my thumbprint. I filled in the paper a little differently from the last time. Instead of *Nie Mowe,* I put *Polski*; I felt I could pass for a Pole with the Russians.

There was a lighter side to those days after the Russians came. The villagers flocked to see me and in nearby villages they would stop me in the road. 'However did you manage it?' was the most usual question. There was embarrassment on some of their faces when they recalled what they'd said in front of me, thinking I couldn't hear. Quite a few blushes from the girls when they realised I knew a few of their secrets.

Another Devil Comes

F ic seemed to be an unpaid liaison officer for the
Russians. Since he could speak their language, they
called on him to find overnight accommodation for the
troops and settle disputes, unless they settled them with
a bullet.

It was a problem keeping the girls out of sight when
the Russians were staying overnight. Fic allocated a
hundred men and perhaps two officers to different
farms in the area. The soldiers allocated to Fic's farm
slept in the barn, but the officers insisted on sleeping in
the house. I slept in the corn store once again, I felt
safer there.

One night when the soldiers had settled down, the
officers had eaten supper and they were talking, there
was a knock at the door. I answered it to a middle-aged
couple. I could tell by their dress that they were
German. I closed the door and ushered them into the
shadow of the outbuildings before I asked them what
they wanted.

'Could we stay the night? The barn, the stable or
anywhere would do,' they pleaded. They were going
back to Germany and had been walking all day.

I told them there were Russian soldiers sleeping in
the barn, but I'd ask if they could sleep in the stable.
They were so grateful when I returned and told them
they could and soon settled down in the stable on some

straw. I took them what the Russians had left from supper, gave them a hot drink, and told them I'd call them when the Russians had gone in the morning.

Everything was quiet when I went to bed in the corn store and I went to sleep. The sound of footsteps woke me. Over the years I'd become very sensitive, the slightest sound and my feet were on the floor. I decided that perhaps the Russians had put a guard on duty and I settled down again. The sounds became too frequent for changing guards, so I decided to have a look to see if the German couple were all right. As soon as I climbed through the trapdoor into the loft, I could see a light shining from the stable. Without making a noise, I crept to the opening above the manger. The lantern hung from a nail in the wall. From its flickering light, I could see the woman lying there wearing very few clothes, a Russian soldier was lying by her side, and there was no sign of her husband. She was crying and moaning, the soldier was talking to her in Russian, and when the door opened, she screamed. The soldier put his hand over her mouth. I felt helpless as the poor woman was raped, as she must have been many times that night. There was the Luger under my pillow, but one shot would bring a hundred Russians swarming out of the barn. I went back to my bed but sleep was impossible. The sound of the continuous change over kept haunting me.

With the first glimmer of daylight, I went to the stable on pretence of feeding the horses. A Russian got up and greeted me with a grunt as he went out, the woman hurriedly dressed. I said I'd fetch her some breakfast, but she shook her head as she stumbled out of the door. She could scarcely walk as she went across the yard and down the drive, sobbing her heart out.

Her husband was lying on a bale of straw in the barn, when I went in. By the look of his face, he'd put up a fight. He jumped up and dashed out when I told him, his wife had gone. I was thankful the Russians didn't try to stop him.

Mietek told how the Russians had begun organising things in Konin. It looked as if they'd come to stay. I thought of Wojciech Rewers when he said, 'We may never be free.'

One of the Russian officers who had stayed overnight sat talking after supper one night. I couldn't resist the temptation to bring up the massacre at Katyn. It was a painful subject in front of Mietek, as his brother was one of the Polish officers. The Russian, who'd had quite a lot to drink, started to explain. The Polish officers were asked to fight on the Russian side as part of their army, but they refused. They agreed to fight, but only under their own flag; this was the last thing the Russians wanted, a Polish army.

'Everything was done to persuade them, but they wouldn't listen,' said the Russian with a shrug of his shoulders.

Mietek's hand gripped the side of the table as he tried to keep calm, 'There was no need to murder them, was there?' he asked.

'What else could we do, when they were so proud?' the Russian asked.

His question remained unanswered as Mietek jumped up and went outside.

Definite news of the war was hard to come by. It was a better army that retreated than the advancing one, but the Germans seemed to have lost the will to fight. We could tell there were still pockets of resistance by the wounded on stretchers that passed by. The Russians had a unique way of bringing back the wounded: dog teams pulled sleighs, with stretchers attached.

One day, on the far side of the village, one of these sleighs appeared. A trail of blood in the snow told me the man on the stretcher was bleeding to death. I knew I couldn't catch them by running after them, but the road through the village wound round like a horseshoe, so I dashed across the fields. I could head them off. I ran in front of the dog team with my arms outstretched. At first, they seemed to hesitate and then the leading dog leapt at me. I saw its teeth flash in my face as I fell backward into the ditch. The sleigh went on with its doomed passenger.

A farmer from the other side of the village ran to the farm one day. He wanted to speak to Fic but he'd gone to Rychwal. The farmer told us the Russians had caught a German prowling round their wagons. Mrs Fic asked me to go back with him; she thought I might be able to help as I could speak a little German by this time. I went on Fic's bicycle and when I arrived the German was standing against the wall of the farmhouse, while a group of Russians were talking about fifteen yards away. The scene seemed to be set for them to shoot him, so I went up to them and asked what he'd done to deserve that. They all stared at me; it was obvious they couldn't speak Polish. One of them shouted to a soldier standing in the doorway of the farmhouse. I saw it was a woman when she came toward us; she looked the type you wanted on your side in a rough house. She acted as interpreter and I discovered the German had tried to steal rations off the wagon, also they didn't think he was as old as he made out to be. Looking at him, I believed they were right – a German soldier, trying to pass as an old man, but that didn't justify shooting him.

'He's an old man, I know him, his two sons were in the army, but he was too old to fight,' I lied.

'He wasn't too old to steal our rations,' the woman said.

'You don't shoot a man for that, give him some whip and let him go.'

She spoke to one of the Russian soldiers and he fetched a whip from the wagon.

As the Russian approached, the German started shouting, 'I've a right. Hitler gave me...,' a shot cut him short.

The woman walked up to him as he lay on the ground, the revolver still in her hand. She spat on him saying, 'That's what Hitler did for you.'

Leaving

On the 6th February, a letter arrived from Alex telling me he had been to the Russian commandant in Konin. Apparently, there had been handshakes all round when Alex had told him who he was. The Russian commandant was arranging for him to be sent to Kutno Aerodrome, flown to Moscow and then home.

Alex then told him about me, and he altered the plan; we both had to report to Konin the following Wednesday. Twice in the letter, Alex emphasised, 'Come to Dziedzice, no later than Monday, without fail.' It certainly was a bombshell.

That same evening, Max arrived with a letter written to him by a friend who had found a job in the Russian commandant's office. It read: *Tell the Englishman who is staying with Franc Fic that his friend came to see the Russian commandant today, and they both have to report here on Wednesday morning.*

What a pity Alex hadn't consulted me, or, since he had such great faith in the Russians, just gone on his own, and conveniently left me out of it. However, the die was cast, and I had two days to say farewell to my friends.

Irena gave me two pictures she'd embroidered on canvas before the war. They were her pride and joy, but she insisted I took them for my wife.

When I arrived at Dziedzice, the house was full of gloom, only Mroz gave me his usual welcome. Mrs Rewers fussed around with coffee and cakes and then Wojciech went to the stables and beckoned me to follow.

His face was tense as he turned to me and said, 'We have helped you for four years. I've lied and done everything I could to stop you from going to Russia.' It was obvious; Alex had gone to Konin against Wojciech's advice, when he said, 'If you must go, for God's sake travel west not east.'

I pointed out to him, if we didn't report as planned, the Russians could pay him and Fic a visit. He seemed relieved when I assured him my way home wasn't via Moscow and I wouldn't go through Russia unless with an organised party.

A smile came to his face as he took a spade and said, 'Come, let's go and dig up Colin Marshall.'

I went to the spot where he'd buried my photograph with the names and addresses of my friends. The ground was too hard, so he fetched a pickaxe saying, 'Tell Alex you can't go until the thaw!'

Another tearful goodbye to Jolanta and Slawek, then Wojciech drove us to Konin, accompanied by his wife. Mrs Rewers had packed a small sack of food; a large piece of ham, butter and three large loaves of bread, enough to last us for weeks.

They wouldn't let Wojciech and his wife go into the commandant's office with us, so we said goodbye to them. The commandant made quite a fuss of us and gave us two lots of papers, one to travel on the train and the other for Kutno aerodrome. Judging by the paperwork, we were going on a world tour.

As we waited at the station for the train, Wojciech and his wife arrived. They'd stayed around to see if it was genuine and we were going to Kutno.

We searched the length of the train, not to sit down, but to get enough room to stand. People were riding on the roof. We turned away with no hope of getting on, and then we heard an American voice shouting, 'Hi there buddies.' Some American soldiers waved frantically from the doorway of a cattle truck attached to the end of the train. We scrambled on and one of the six Americans asked, 'Where are you bound for?'

'Kutno,' said Alex.

'Warsaw,' said I.

'I thought we were going to Kutno and then on to Moscow. We have the papers,' said Alex, with a puzzled look.

'My way home isn't via Moscow. I'm going to Warsaw to see if we've anyone representing us there. I don't intend going through Russia unless it's with an organised party.'

The train passed through Kola. My thoughts went back a few months. It was there where Irena was at the camp. So many things had happened since I took her home on the crossbar of the bicycle.

A voice behind me interrupted my thoughts. It was a woman's voice saying, 'Excuse me, are you Polish?' I explained I was a POW on my way home. While we talked, the train stopped at Kutno station. Alex just sat there. I didn't speak; I didn't want to influence him, one way or the other.

As the train left the station, I asked Alex if he wanted something to eat. I explained to the Americans that we hadn't had anything to eat since breakfast. One of them spoke up; he seemed to be the joker of the pack.

'Please Mister, don't start eating in front of me, my stomach wouldn't stand it.'

'Haven't you had anything to eat today?' I asked.

'Today!' he exclaimed, 'I haven't eaten since Monday.'

There wasn't a crumb left by the time they'd finished. I had no regrets; I knew what it was to be hungry. Before we arrived in Warsaw, the woman sitting behind me gave me a slip of paper. 'If you need help or somewhere to stay, contact this address.'

We must have looked a motley crowd, walking through Warsaw. There were many curious glances. We stopped a passer-by and asked if he knew of any representatives for English or American soldiers. He said he thought there was a camp for American POWs and he gave us directions. I took one look at the camp with its barbed wire and Russian guards and decided that wasn't for me. After a little consultation, the Americans followed saying, 'We don't like the look of that set up either.'

I took the scrap of paper out of my pocket and asked a man in the street if he could direct us. He told us it was only a short distance away and he escorted us to the place.

It was a large block of flats and having thanked our escort, we started looking for the number. A man opened the door and asked in Polish what we wanted. Then he saw the American uniforms; he stepped to one side saying in perfect English, 'Come in my friends.'

When we sat down, I asked him if our government had any representatives in Warsaw. He waved the question aside saying, we eat first, talk later.

Eight of us sat down to a meal, six Americans, Alex and me. I felt uncomfortable; I asked our host why they weren't joining us.

'We can't afford to eat like this, but you are our special guests.'

After the meal was over our host, who had introduced himself as Bolesz, kept looking at his watch. He was obviously expecting someone. There was a knock on the door and he hurried to open it saying, 'Here is Sigmund!' Perhaps it was a coincidence, but I could have sworn the knock on the door sounded like a 'Z' in Morse code. The newcomer, introduced to us just as Sigmund, spoke Polish and apologised for not speaking in English. He said he wasn't as clever as the others were, but he was being modest, he looked and spoke like a leader. I felt he'd been a high-ranking officer; his voice was both determined and bitter. After a consultation with Sigmund, Bolesz told us there were no Allied representatives in Warsaw; the Germans had transferred the Government to Lublin. There was a French representative there, but he was from the Vichy Government. He said our best plan was to go to Lublin, because if there were any organised repatriation, it would be from there.

'Sigmund has made arrangements. Stay with us until tomorrow evening and then we shall put you on the road to Lublin, where a lorry will drive alongside you. Wave your hand and it will stop; then ask for a ride to Lublin. There will be two Russians in the cab, but one of them has a Polish heart. Remember don't have any conversation with them.'

It took a weight off our minds having things organised for us. We could relax and talk to these friendly people, and the conversation turned to Warsaw. I asked him if he was disappointed that my country didn't help more.

He put his hand on my shoulder and said, 'No one can do the impossible.' His next statement gave me the impression he was one of the leaders when he said, 'We had word from London that the time was right. They would give us all the help they could and reminded us the Russians were just across the river. What a tragedy! The Russians stayed where they were, across the river. Moreover, they refused to let your planes land to refuel. Without that help it was suicide.' I thought he was going to talk more about it, but he just sadly shook his head and said, 'Very few of us survived. I was married in the sewers of Warsaw, when we thought our days were numbered.'

Later Sigmund bid us goodbye, taking the six Americans with him.

Alex and I stayed with Bolesz, he talked late into the night about his work and the war. He was a secretary to Colonel Beck, a minister in the Polish Government before the war. We were just settling down to sleep when a woman's scream, coming from the flat above, caused us to jump to our feet. We rushed upstairs to find a woman cowering in a corner, screaming. Her face was a terrible mess; a man in uniform was beating a child in the other corner. I thought that he was a Russian soldier who was molesting them. Grabbing hold of him, I banged his head against the wall and kept on banging it until Bolesz stopped me. When the woman calmed down she told us what had happened.

Her husband had been a POW in Russia and had just come home. He had obviously been brainwashed, because after having some drink, he started talking to them in Russian. When they didn't understand and answered in Polish, he went berserk and started beating them saying, 'Nothing is Polish now; everything is Russian.'

The husband lay on the bed moaning, Bolesz went to him and had a few words, then he told the woman to fetch us if she had any more trouble. As we went downstairs Bolesz said, 'I don't think she will have any more trouble after the way you bashed his head against the wall.'

The Americans returned after breakfast and we spent the whole day in the flat. Quite a few Russian soldiers were patrolling the streets.

When we said goodbye, Bolesz's wife gave me a small piece of paper with a name and address of a woman in Lublin. It was her sister's address. The paper was so small I could hardly read it.

'Go there if you need help, but if you are arrested put it in your mouth and swallow it.'

I smiled; at least it would be easier to swallow than my identity paper.

Bolesz put the eight of us on the road to Lublin and bid us goodbye and good luck. We had not gone far when we heard a lorry approaching from behind, we waved and it pulled up. I asked in Polish if he would give us a lift to Lublin. There was a conversation in Russian between the two men in the cab. The driver told us to jump in the back and off we went.

Lublin was about 160 kilometres from Warsaw, but it seemed like 300. The driver was pulled up three times, but it wasn't for speeding. Russian soldiers stopped him and checked his papers, but they didn't come and look in the back. We rumbled to a halt just outside Lublin. I thought it was another checkpoint until the driver knocked on the back of his cab and told us to get out.

We passed a small farm and I suggested we hide in the barn as we would look suspicious characters walking through the town at that unearthly hour.

The farmer was surprised when he found us in the morning. He insisted we breakfasted with him; it was *kasha*, like our porridge. The Americans didn't think much to it, but Alex and I were used to it. One thing in its favour – it was steaming hot. The farmer said he didn't think there were any Western representatives in Lublin, apart from the French.

When we reached the town of Lublin, I recognised the name of the street on the bit of paper in my pocket. We knocked on the door of a large house, halfway down the street. A refined looking lady opened the door. When she saw us she gasped, 'My God!' and clutched the door for support, her face ashen.

'Don't worry, we're friends. We are English.'

Tears of relief ran down her cheeks as she beckoned us to enter. She sat on a settee and after a few minutes, composed herself and said, 'When I saw you, I thought they'd come.'

No need to ask who, so instead I asked, 'Why should they come?'

She spoke as someone resigned to fate, 'My husband is a doctor and they are short of doctors, so I live in fear.'

She jumped up apologising for her inhospitality and hurried to the kitchen, she returned with coffee and cakes. The Americans were soon murmuring their approval. When I stood up and said we would have to be going, she insisted we stay for dinner, to meet her husband. I told her we were anxious to find if there was anything being organised for our repatriation.

'Don't worry. After dinner I'll take you to someone who will look after you and she is English.'

Her husband came home; he looked a typical doctor, with his pleasant, open face. The type you could tell all your troubles to, but once or twice during dinner, he looked to have enough troubles of his own. His wife told him of the scare she'd had when we appeared at the door. I asked if he feared being sent to the front.

'No chance. I'd welcome that. But Siberia is where they need doctors,' he said.

The Americans chorused, 'They can't send you there against your will.'

He replied meekly, 'You have faith in justice. It's different here. It's not my will that counts, it's theirs.'

We insisted on washing up after dinner and then she took us to the person who was to be our benefactor.

Before we left, her husband shook hands with us, saying, 'I must say goodbye. I may see you tomorrow or I may not. That's my life now.'

Alex and I walked with the lady. The Americans followed behind since they wore uniforms. She pointed to a small school, 'That's where our friend is staying.'

A woman answered the door. Her Polish was perfect as the two ladies greeted each other and so was her English when she greeted us with, 'Come on inside boys and welcome home.' When I crossed the doorstep, I felt I had one foot in England.

The doctor's wife soon made her departure; she was worried to death about her husband. Our host told us, before we settled down, that she had some work for us.

She took us to a shed at the back of the school, which was filled with bales of straw and a pile of palliasses. 'Fill one each and bring them back to the house.'

Later we placed the eight mattresses side by side in a small classroom.

It was hard to believe what this woman told us, as she explained her presence here in enemy territory, a thousand miles from home. First, she'd run a hostel for German officers on their way to and from the Eastern front. Later she took over the school as well; this was also used as a temporary accommodation for the Germans. 'You would be surprised what information you can get out of a tired German.'

Mrs Smith was the name by which she chose to be known, and no one questioned it. She suggested we turn in early, as the Russians would investigate if they saw lights in the school. She admitted she was at a loss to understand the Russian attitude and warned us never to be on our own.

Next morning we had to return our bedding to the store, and then having washed, Mrs Smith informed us that the doctor's wife was expecting us for breakfast.

The moment she opened the door, we knew her husband had been taken, her face was deathly white, her eyes red and swollen.

'When did they take him?' we all asked the question together.

'Three o'clock this morning. He is at the police station. I've taken him some breakfast, they don't provide food. They said he would be charged tomorrow, but they wouldn't say what for.'

She then gave Alex and me some advice, 'For God's sake, get into some kind of uniform.' There was wisdom in her words, but uniforms were hard to come by.

That afternoon there was a flood of POWs to the schoolhouse, English, American and French. Mrs Smith was at her wits' end where to put everyone. The straw had all gone and she asked me to go to the kitchen and tell Henryk, her caretaker, to fetch some more. I'd almost reached the kitchen door when a man came out carrying a bucket. He stared at me as though I was a ghost and he let the bucket fall, buried his head in his hands, and sobbed. I wondered what was wrong with him as I ran and fetched Mrs Smith.

'I think you had better go back to your friends, I'll explain later,' she said.

That left me more puzzled than ever. Everyone had been fixed up with bedding when she called me into the kitchen. Henryk came and offered his hand, saying he was sorry; I shook his hand still puzzled. Later I asked Mrs Smith and she explained: when she first took over the school, one of her countrymen was brought to her. She looked after him for many months, until it was possible to get him away. Henryk's wife was very kind to him, bringing him home-baked cakes and cigarettes. He often said he would remember her after the war. They must have put him in touch with the underground and on the day he left, he was warned not to carry anything that could be traced back to his benefactors. One day the Gestapo arrived with a small piece of paper with a name and address of the caretaker's wife on it. It was rumoured they shot her, no one saw her again, she just disappeared.

There was a silence, until I asked what had this to do with me?

'When you first arrived at this house I could have sworn it was the man we helped, at first glance you are his double. I didn't expect Henryk to act as he did. You are lucky he didn't crash that bucket on your head.'

Next morning the Americans accompanied Alex and me to the doctor's house, and some friends of the doctor and his wife were there when we arrived. They told us the doctor's wife had taken her husband's breakfast to the police station but he wasn't there. Someone had seen him enter the railway station walking between two Russian soldiers. She was too distressed to see us, but as we stood up to leave, she entered the room. She gave me a sheet of paper and said, 'That's the address of the Red Cross. Go there and they will give you some money. Perhaps you'll be able to buy food.'

'Is there any way we can help you?' I asked before we left.

'No one can help me now, only God,' she replied.

We made our way to the address, not that I thought money would buy much. A pound of butter would buy more than a sack full of money. The Polish Red Cross were only too pleased to give us a grant of money. The only commodity they had plenty of was money; food and clothing seemed to be out of the question, they were near starvation themselves. We received five hundred marks each, it seemed a princely sum, but it didn't buy a thing. A barter system was operating; for articles of clothing, you could get food.

At midday, the Red Cross delivered soup with potatoes boiled in their jackets. As more of our fellows arrived, the soup was watered down, but what else could they do?

Mrs Smith once more begged me to get into some kind of uniform and I promised I'd try but it was easier said than done. Fortunately, Alex had his khaki tunic and trousers in his briefcase, so he was equipped. My countrymen, who did have spare clothing, had found out they could be bartered for food. The six Americans went out to search and returned with a shirt, a pullover and trousers, all American army issue. I wanted a tunic and overcoat, but no one seemed to have those to spare. We asked everyone throughout the school, but no one had a spare overcoat.

A Frenchman passed by wearing an overcoat and with another draped over his arm. One of the Americans could speak French, so with his aid I swapped my civilian overcoat for his threadbare spare one. Dressed in the American shirt and trousers, complete with a threadbare French overcoat, I went to get Mrs Smith's approval. She burst out laughing when she saw me and then she added, 'Well, at least you don't look so conspicuous now.'

After dinner that day, a group of Russian officers visited Mrs Smith. When she'd seen them off, she returned smiling. 'Some good news for you boys, you leave for home tomorrow,' she said amid the cheers.

During the afternoon, we went round saying our goodbyes to the acquaintances we'd made. The news had soon got round we were leaving. People were shaking hands in the streets.

We were on the station at nine o'clock when our train arrived. There were three carriages at the front, followed by cattle trucks. Some of our fellows made a dive for the carriages, but the Russian guards fetched them out. I don't know where the train had started from, but some of the trucks were already filled with ex-POWs, some from Lodz and Krakow. The guards arrived and counted us, fifty to a cattle truck, just enough room to sit down with knees under your chin. With a roar and a wave from the Polish crowd, the train moved out.

The sliding doors on the trucks had a lock and chain, so they could be opened about eighteen inches and no more. At first, we thought it was for ventilation until the train went on for hours and hours without stopping. Then we realised it was for other purposes, the chain was used as a toilet seat.

Once during the day, the train stopped and the trucks were uncoupled and shunted onto the back of a goods train and off we went again. They put two buckets of water in each truck and two enamel mugs; there was no sign of food. It was the middle of February and bitterly cold. The threadbare overcoat kept as much cold out as a spider's web. The truck doors were kept shut unless it was a dire emergency.

We ground to a halt the following morning. When we opened the door there was a large building alongside the track, apart from that it looked like a wilderness. The water buckets were refilled and a huge sack of dry rations thrown in each truck. It was bread, which had been sliced, then dipped in fish oil and fried until it was as hard as rock. The smell put off many of us, others tried it, but very few ate it. One of them who did was sick before he reached the door. We were ravenous, yet we couldn't face that bread.

On the third morning, we stopped and they brought water, but nothing else. Three Russian officers walked along the line; one of them was of high rank, according to the red braid he was wearing. When they reached our truck, he pointed to his mouth and then the sack, he was wondering why we'd not eaten. I knew a few words of Russian from hearing Fic speak, so I told him it was no good.

'If we don't have something to eat soon, you'll have some sick or dead men on your hands.' I was hoping one of them might understand Polish. One of them stepped closer.

'Didn't you have anything to eat yesterday?' he asked in a mixture of Polish and Russian.

'Not yesterday or the day before and today will make three,' I answered and held up three fingers, so that he would get the message. He passed the information on to his senior and they had a discussion. The one who had spoken in Polish turned to us and said, 'You will get a good meal tonight, we will make arrangements.'

Stations seemed few and far between in this part of the world; it seemed to be in the middle of nowhere. It was getting late, the promise of a good meal looked empty, some of the lads said I must have misunderstood; the good meal was tomorrow night.

In the middle of this bantering, the train stopped and we looked out to see men walking about with lanterns. One of them walked along the line, unlocked the chains, and opened the doors. We were hustled into a building, which looked like a school, with four big rooms and some outbuildings. From these buildings wafted a lovely smell of soup, it made us want to dive for it.

It was a candle lit supper, that was their only lighting, but a huge bowl of soup and a chunk of rye bread made up for the decor. It was a bit awkward with clumsy wooden spoons, but I never heard a grumble. One of the men serving warned us that it was hot; somehow, it was natural to repeat it in Polish. He asked if I was Polish and I shook my head, I was too busy with the soup to talk.

After supper, they asked if anyone smoked; these men were given a piece of newspaper and some home-grown tobacco. I moved into a corner to get away from the smoke. Later the man who had served me with the soup joined me. He was dying to hold a conversation and the smoke-filled room gave him the chance. I asked where he'd learnt Polish. He said he'd served in the army and had learnt Polish and Rumanian there. I asked him a question I'd wanted to ask for years.

'Are you better off now than when the Czar was here?' I asked.

After a furtive look round, he answered, 'Just the same.' He pointed to one of the Russian soldiers saying, 'They are better off, we're not. We are like horses, work, eat and sleep. If you don't go to listen to the news bulletin, they accuse you of not being a good citizen. If you refuse to do a job of work, or you say anything wrong about the boss or a government official, the charge is working against the State. You can go to Siberia for that.'

He stood up and held out his hand, 'Forget what I've told you Mister and goodbye.'

I had my answer from a working-man in the middle of nowhere; I'll never forget it.

When we returned to the truck, a man offered us five small loaves for the sack of dry rations. He waved to us as we left, so pleased with his bargain, and we were satisfied, a loaf between ten of us was better than none. The train rattled on through the night, there seemed to be no hurry.

In the morning, the soldiers filled the buckets with water but there was no food; perhaps they thought we'd over-eaten the previous night. There was a surprise at midday, when we pulled into a small station. They brought baskets of bread and threw ten loaves into each truck and the train was on the move again. Somehow, I thought we were an embarrassment to them. They wanted us out of the way as soon as possible. Things were getting better, a loaf between five, that was two slices of dry bread and water for the day. It was also starting to get a little warmer.

Early on the fifth morning, we arrived in Odessa. The guards lost no time forming us into lines and marching us a short distance to either a school or a college of some sort. We had a Russian style breakfast, borsch and potatoes.

Then in parties of about thirty, we were escorted down to the communal showers. One of the men told us what would happen.

'Place your clothes in a basket as you enter the baths; they will be fumigated. Then you will be handed a small piece of soap as you enter the shower room.'

I was very pleased the man gave us that information about the showers, as I still had the German Luger in my shirt and I put it behind a bucket in a washroom before the shower, hoping no one would find it.

We found that the water from the showers was a trickle, sometimes too hot, mostly too cold, but it certainly made us feel and smell better. After five days in a cattle truck, we smelt like cattle.

Dinner was vegetable soup, ten turnips to one ounce of meat. What did it matter, the news we'd just heard was more fulfilling than the meal; three British ships were standing out at sea, awaiting permission to land.

During the afternoon, a Russian officer arrived with an interpreter. He explained that before we could leave we had to be registered. To save time he told us the order in which he wanted our particulars when we filed past a table next morning – number, name, rank, regiment and home address.

That little briefing gave someone cold feet, for a little later a man asked me if I could speak Polish. When I said I could, he asked if I'd go with him and explain to a Polish man in their company, that they could no longer take him with them.

I couldn't believe my ears, 'Do you mean to say you've brought a Pole all this way into Russia, and now you are going to dump him?'

'What else can we do?' he answered lamely.

The Polish man was sitting at a table with four English men. He looked scared as he was beginning to understand what they were trying to say. He looked so relieved when I spoke to him in Polish. He clutched my arm, saying, 'Tell them, if they leave me here Mister, the Russians will shoot me.' I asked him how he came to be there in the first place. He explained he'd met the four Englishmen near the German border. Although he couldn't speak English, they'd made a bargain, if he took them to Lublin they would take him back to England with them. The four of them looked shamefaced as they said, 'You can't expect us to take him now, can you?'

'You can't take him, but you could have left him on his own soil in Lublin. There's only one thing I want you to do now. Keep your mouths shut and forget you ever saw this man.' I left them, taking the Pole with me. It's strange to say, I never saw any of them again.

After explaining to my new friend about the register, I wrote on a piece of paper a bogus number, name, rank, regiment and address. I chose names that I could write with Polish phonetics, so that he could pronounce them without needing to know the meaning. My nephew's name came in handy, John Fox - he pronounced it almost perfectly when I wrote, 'Dzon Foks'. I had to tell him not to put too much emphasis on the letter 's' at the end of Foks. Very soon, he could say all I'd wrote on the paper, but he had to learn it off by heart. We spent hours that night learning it, until it made his head ache. I reminded him if he didn't get it perfect, the Russians would stop his headache with a bullet.

I had to smile when I woke next morning; he was repeating his particulars over and over again. As we filed past the table that morning, I stood behind him; I thought if he made a slip, I could probably cover up for him. I'd told him to pause after each part while the man wrote it down, and in practice, he'd done this.

He rattled the whole thing off like a piece of poetry but the man writing the details had only got the first three numbers. Realising what he'd done, he started again pausing till the man stopped writing then going on again.

The Pole was as pleased as someone who had passed for university. 'Shall I be able to go now?' he asked.

I told him the only danger would be if the interpreter spoke to him in English. 'If he does, don't make a sign that you've heard him and I'll explain you are deaf.'

What a feeling of relief when I reached the top of the gangway of the 'Empress of Britain', I felt like kneeling down and kissing the deck. There was quite a bit of pushing and I lost sight of my friend, but it didn't matter now, he was safe on board ship. We were taken to our quarters and left to settle in. Later, I made my way up the decks again; I wanted to see our final departure.

Safe At Last

The sirens wailed, the ropes cast off and I could feel the ship moving. At last, I was on my way home. What am I going to find at home? I'd been as good as dead for nearly five years. Kaszmira's words came to my mind, 'Perhaps she's found someone else.' My God, I thought, she may be married. I stood holding on to the rails, trying to collect my thoughts. I put my hand in my shirt, pulled out the Luger, and flung it into the sea. If there is someone else in her life, I'll walk out of it.

As I went down the steps to E-deck, I met my Polish friend.

'I've been looking for you,' he said. 'What shall I tell them when they ask my name? Shall I say, *Dzon Foks*?'

I forgot my problems as I laughed and said, 'If you like you can tell them you are Marshal Pilsudski. You are in England now, or as good as.'

Epilogue

M y father's ship sailed on through the Dardanelles to the Mediterranean and called at Naples, which allowed the six Americans to disembark. The falsely named John Fox (Dzon Foks) also disembarked as the ship's captain thought it best for him to join the Polish Army in Italy, hopefully to start a new life in freedom. Once back in England, my father spent some time in Chester Military Hospital, recovering from his ordeal.

My mother, Nancy, spent the war working in Blackpool at a Convalescence Centre for the Royal Air Force, based at the Russell Hotel and then the Nolan Hotel. She received POW cards from my father, Colin, until December 1940, but when reported as missing, she had no contact with him again until March 1945. She never gave up hope that she would see her husband again and they were reunited in March 1945 at Chester Military Hospital.

Dad never forgot his Polish friends and in August 1961, my mother and I, aged eleven years old, accompanied him on a visit to Poland, where we visited Wojciech's farm. We had an emotional welcome from the Rewers family and they invited the Fic family to their farm for a reunion.

Later, the now grown-up Slawek offered to take Dad to Modlibogowice on his motorcycle. The journey revived a lot of memories: the bridge over the Warte; Zagorow, the small town from where the Jews disappeared overnight and the police headquarters at Trabczyn, the place that brought a cold sweat to Dad's brow on many occasions.

Everyone in those Polish villages instantly recognised Dad; they still remembered Stefan Wysocki - *Nie mowe*.

Documents And Photographs

Photograph of Colin Marshall in army uniform, 1930s.

Photograph of Nancy Cheetham at Warehouseman &
Clerks School, Cheadlehulme, Manchester - 1930s.

Colin and Nancy, 1936.

Kriegsgefangenenlager
Stalag XXI B

Datum 17-6-40

Darling, I am alright so dont worry, still terribly in love and longing to come home. Keep things going and look after yourself. Send me a tin of Treacle and Chocolate you must enquire at Chesterfield GPO for instructions. Never forget Your (Take this card) Loving Husband
Colin X X X X

Kriegsgefangenenlager

Datum 9/7/1940

My Darling Wife
I'm well treated and in good health always thinking and longing for you dear. Write me some long letters but if you send parcel dont put a letter in. Loving you always. please dont forget
Your Loving Husband
Colin X X X X

POW cards June and July 1940 from Colin – Stalag XXIB.

My Dear Wife

15ᵗ Sept

I'm still looking forward to a letter dear for though I haven't received one I know you will have wrote I'm always with you in my thoughts. Nancy I long for the day we really are together forever! Tell me all about yourself when you write dear never mind Mrs Soᵈsoᵉ's new hat. I just long to know you are safe & well and more so that your still caring There is a fellow from Clowne here and we spend most of our spare time talking of home and people we know, its good to talk of places so near and think of the happy hours you & I have spent there I wonder what its like to stroll down Elmton. Well sweetheart the space is small so keep hoping and thinking of me. I'll come back to you one day darling, changed perhaps but for the better Regards to Mother & Dad. Hope they are well

Ever Lasting Love Your Loving
Husband Colin

POW letter from Colin – Stalag XXIB.

POW card from Colin dated 6.12.1940. Colin wrote
this on the day of the escape. The quote: *Remember the
platform ticket,* was a hint to Nancy that he was going to
attempt an escape.

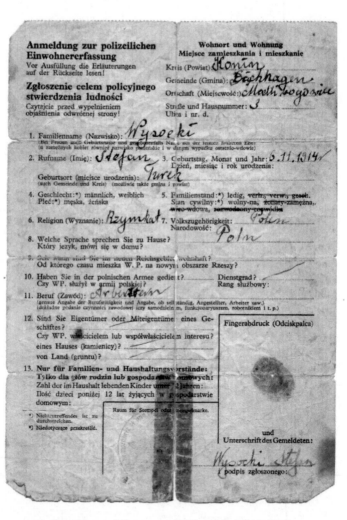

Stefan Wysocki's second Identification Paper.

Dear Colin —

I am at the moment in Konin. Today I visited the Russian Commandant of Konin and explained the ~~whole story~~. Sufficient proof was available to ascertain our identity. I did not tell him about you until I was sure everything was O.K. He said that I would go by lorry to Kolo and be in Moscow today being taken by plane. When I told him about you he said we would travel together! I have arranged with him for us to appear here in Konin on Wednesday. Drop everything and come to Dziedzie at once. Monday I shall expect you because I am not sure that you will get this. Be sure to come on Monday. Otherwise I will think you have not received this letter. Don't fail me. Get here on Monday. Give my regards all round. We go by plane to the English Consul. Alex

Letter from Alex Jenkins dated 6.2.1945.

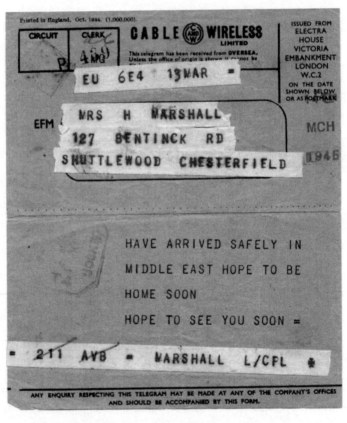

Colin's telegram dated 13.3.1945.

In reply please
quote C2/11M.

Royal Engineers Record Office,
Ditchling Road,
Brighton, Sussex.

12 April 1945.

Dear Madam,

No 4800080 A/L/Cpl Marshall C.R.

With further reference to the
communication from this office dated 9th March
last, I now have to inform you that a report has
been received stating that your Husband, the
above named Non Commissioned Officer, arrived in
this country and was admitted to Chester Military
Hospital on 30th March 1945.

In congratulating you upon the safe
return home of your Husband from enemy territory,
I would express the hope that he will make rapid
recovery from the effects of his experiences while
prisoner of war and escapee.

Yours faithfully,

Colonel,
Officer i/c RE Records.

Mrs H. Marshall,
127 Bentinck Road,
Shuttlewood,
Nr. Chesterfield,
DERBYSHIRE.

MC.

Letter from Regiment dated 12.4.1945.

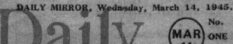

DAILY MIRROR, Wednesday, March 14, 1945.

Daily Mirror

MAR 14

No. 12,865
ONE PENNY
Registered
at the G.P.O.
as
a Newspaper.

✦ ✦ ✦ ✦

Briton posed as a deaf mute, beat Hun

3 years

FOR over three years a British soldier who escaped from a German prisoners of war camp posed successfully as a deaf and dumb Pole in German-occupied

He is Lance-Corporal Colin Marshall, of the Royal Engineers, whose wife lives at 56, Clown-road, Stanfree, near Chesterfield.

He is recovering from his ordeal in the hospital of the ship which arrived at a Middle East port on Monday from Odessa with over 1,700 Allied war prisoners liberated by the Red Army.

Also in hospital on board with him—neither is really ill—is another British soldier who escaped with Marshall, was recaptured, but returned to Poland after escaping a second time and found Marshall posing as a mute

He is Driver Alexander Jenkins, 27, whose wife and son, after losing their Liverpool home through enemy action, now reside at Rockingham-road, Kettering, Northants.

He described how he and Marshall and another soldier escaped in December, 1940, but were caught by the winter in Poland.

When the thaw came they cut cards as to who should go on and Marshall was left behind.

Jenkins was recaptured, but escaped again in September of last year.

In civilian clothes, and a Homburg hat which he "pinched" in a beer hall, he made his way by train and on foot to the district where he had left Marshall.

"I found him about 10 miles from where I had left him," said Jenkins. "He was posing as a mute with complete success.

"Last month we heard that a Russian mobile column had passed through the district where we were and, after waiting for a few days, we set off on our travels again and reached Lublin

Newspaper Report. © Mirrorpix.

Photograph of Hazel with her dad, 1960.